Analytic Geometry and Vectors

Analytic Geometry and Vectors

J. Hunter

In association with
The Scottish Mathematics Group

Blackie Glasgow and London
Chambers Edinburgh and London

Blackie & Son Limited Bishopbriggs, Glasgow G64 2NZ
7 Leicester Place, London WC2H 7BP

W. & R. Chambers Limited 43–5 Annandale Street, Edinburgh EH7 4AZ

First published 1972
Reprinted 1972, 1975, 1980, 1981, 1982, 1985

Blackie Educational Edition 0 216 87720 2
Chambers Educational Edition 0 550 75892 5

Printed in Great Britain by Thomson Litho Ltd, East Kilbride, Scotland

Preface

The aim of this book is to cover the basic work in plane and 3-dimensional analytic geometry that may be regarded as essential for mathematics and its applications. In particular the book covers most of the geometry required for Paper II of the Scottish Sixth Year Studies Examination in Mathematics and it should be useful not only for study at the Advanced Level of the General Certificate of Education, but also for certain courses in Colleges of Education and Universities.

Part 1 on plane geometry introduces geometrical notation used throughout the book. Although this part should not be used for a first introduction to plane analytic geometry, it should be useful in consolidating important parts of the work. Vectors have not been used here since it is felt that they are most effective in 3-dimensional space; in any case the x, y-plane can be "imbedded" in x, y, z-space by "identifying" the vector (x, y) with the vector $(x, y, 0)$. The problems listed in Exercise **1** should be regarded as an integral part of the text. They are listed in the order in which the topics are covered, ending with conics.

Part 2 consists of 3-dimensional analytic geometry with work on vectors built into it in order to deal with directions. In geometry a vector is often defined as a translation; this definition has been avoided here since at this stage the student may well be meeting vectors in Physics. To simplify language a vector is often identified in the book with a line-segment representing it; e.g. the statement: "Plane π contains vector $\boldsymbol{a}$" is a short-hand version for the statement: "There is a line-segment, representing vector $\boldsymbol{a}$, which lies in plane π." Again the main exercise, Exercise **2**, should be used as an integral part of the text.

Although the approach used in the text is through intuitive geometrical thinking, the ideas covered and the language used are not only important in themselves and for applications but lead on to the next mathematical stage when the abstract concept of a vector space will be introduced.

Contents

Part 1 The euclidean plane		
Introduction	Sect. 1	page 3
Coordinates in a plane	2	5
Subsets of the plane, locus	3	10
Some examples illustrating various techniques	4	12
Half-planes, linear programming	5	16
Change of coordinates	6	19
Some geometrical transformations	7	21
Introduction to conics	8	26
Exercise 1		38
Part 2 Three-dimensional geometry		
Coordinates in 3-dimensional euclidean space	1	45
Some simple loci in space	2	48
Vectors	3	51
Geometrical applications of addition and scalar multiples of vectors	4	55
Scalar product and vector product of vectors	5	67
Applications in geometry of scalar and vector products	6	74
Worked examples on lines and planes	7	77
Coordinate systems	8	81
Some simple surfaces	9	83
Exercise 2		87
Answers		95
Index		101

Part 1

The Euclidean Plane

The Euclidean Plane

I

1. Introduction, coordinates on a line

It will be assumed that the student has already been introduced to plane analytical geometry. Consequently this chapter contains merely a survey of some aspects of this work including a brief discussion of the plane curves called conics. Some of the notation to be used in the geometry will be described in the introduction of coordinates on a line.

If A, B are points on a line, $\vec{AB}$ will denote the **line-segment** of the line *from* A *to* B; then $\vec{BA}$ is the line-segment *from* B *to* A. $\vec{AB}$ and $\vec{BA}$ denote the same set of points, but oriented in opposite directions.

$|\vec{AB}|$ or $|AB|$ will denote the non-negative real number which gives the measure of the length of the line-segment from A to B in terms of a given unit of length; then $|AB| = |BA|$.

A **directed line** is a line whose directions are distinguished by calling one positive and the other negative, the positive direction being indicated, as in the diagram, by an arrowhead.

If $\vec{AB}$ is a line-segment of a directed line, we shall write

$$AB = \begin{cases} |AB| \text{ if } \vec{AB} \text{ is in the positive direction,} \\ -|AB| \text{ if } \vec{AB} \text{ is in the negative direction.} \end{cases}$$

The real number AB is called the **measure** of $\vec{AB}$ on the directed line; AB is positive or negative according as $\vec{AB}$ is in the positive or negative direction and $AA = |AA| = 0$.

Since $\vec{AB}$ and $\vec{BA}$ are in opposite directions, it follows that

$$AB = -BA.$$

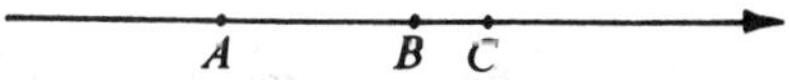

If A, B, C are points on a line, we define an addition of line-segments $\vec{AB}$, $\vec{BC}$ by writing

$$\vec{AB} + \vec{BC} = \vec{AC}.$$

An obvious question that arises is: "If the line is directed, does the equation $AB+BC=AC$ hold?" In fact, it does and forms a key result in the setting up of coordinates.

Theorem 1.1. *For all points A, B, C of a directed line,*

$$AB+BC=AC. \tag{1.1}$$

Proof. The result is easily checked for the cases in which A, B, C are not distinct.

When A, B, C are distinct we verify the result from a diagram for each of the six possible cases arising from the direction of $\overrightarrow{AC}$ and the position of B relative to A and C:

$\overrightarrow{AC}$ in positive direction $\qquad$ $\overrightarrow{AC}$ in negative direction

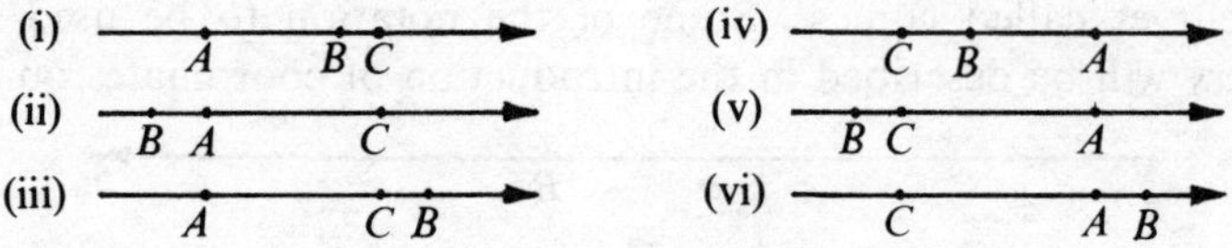

It should be noted that the corresponding statement involving distances, namely $|AB|+|BC|=|AC|$, is not always true; it holds if and only if B belongs to the line-segment $\overrightarrow{AC}$.

Coordinates on a line

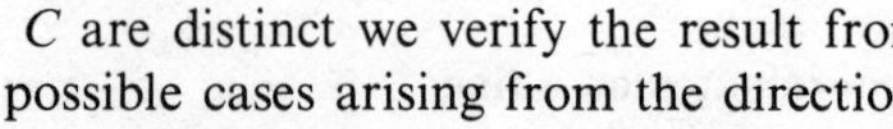

Let us choose one direction of the line as positive direction and denote this direction, as indicated, by $x'x$; we take a point O on the line and a given unit of length. The point A on the line such that $OA=1$ is at unit distance from O in the positive direction.

If P is a point on the line and if $OP=x$, then x is called the x-**coordinate** of P in the **coordinate system** determined by **axis** $x'x$, **origin** O, and given unit of length.

The mapping f: line$\to\mathbf{R}$ defined by $f(P)=x$ is a bijection, i.e. a one-one mapping of the set of points on the line to $\mathbf{R}$, the set of real numbers. This is one of the basic assumptions that we make for euclidean space.

The x-coordinate of P is often denoted by x_P or p.

Theorem 1.2. *If A, B are points on the line $x'x$, then*

$$AB=x_B-x_A.$$

Proof. $AB = AO + OB = -OA + OB = OB - OA = x_B - x_A$. (1.2)

Example. Show that, if $A_1, A_2, \ldots, A_n$ are points on a directed line, then $A_1A_2 + A_2A_3 + \ldots + A_{n-1}A_n = A_1A_n$.

Proof. If O is any point on the line, then, by the argument used for (1.2),

$$\begin{aligned} A_1A_2 + A_2A_3 + \ldots + A_{n-1}A_n = \quad & OA_2 - OA_1 \quad = OA_n - OA_1 = A_1A_n. \\ & + OA_3 - OA_2 \\ & + \ldots\ldots\ldots \\ & \ldots\ldots\ldots\ldots \\ & + OA_n - OA_{n-1} \end{aligned}$$

2. Coordinates in a plane

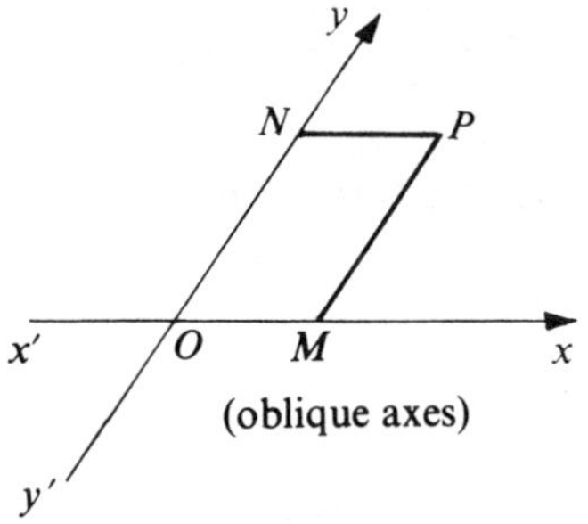

(oblique axes)

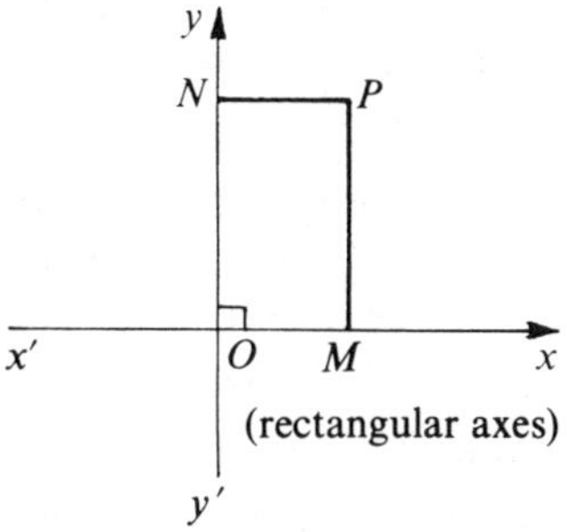

(rectangular axes)

We take directed lines $x'x$ and $y'y$ in the plane intersecting at a point O and such that $\angle xOy$ is positive, i.e. counterclockwise, and choose a unit of length. If, as shown in the diagrams, PM and PN are the parallels through a point P in the plane to $y'y$ and $x'x$ and if $OM = x$ and $ON = y$, then x, y are called the x- and y-**coordinates** of P in the **coordinate system** consisting of x-**axis** $x'x$, y-**axis** $y'y$, **origin** O and given unit of length. We say that P is the point with coordinates (x, y).

By the basic assumptions for euclidean space there is a bijection from the plane to $\mathbf{R}^2 = \{(x, y) : x \in \mathbf{R}, y \in \mathbf{R}\}$, i.e. the set of all ordered pairs of real numbers, by mapping the point P to (x, y).

When $\angle xOy = \frac{1}{2}\pi$ (radians), the axes are said to be **rectangular**; when $\angle xOy \neq \frac{1}{2}\pi$, the axes are called **oblique axes.**

Since most formulae in analytical geometry are simpler when rectangular axes are used, we shall normally use rectangular axes. Such axes divide the plane into four regions called **quadrants** (excluding the axes themselves).

The quadrants determined by angles xOy, yOx', $x'Oy'$, $y'Ox$ are called the first, second, third and fourth quadrants, respectively.

Distance formula (for rectangular axes).

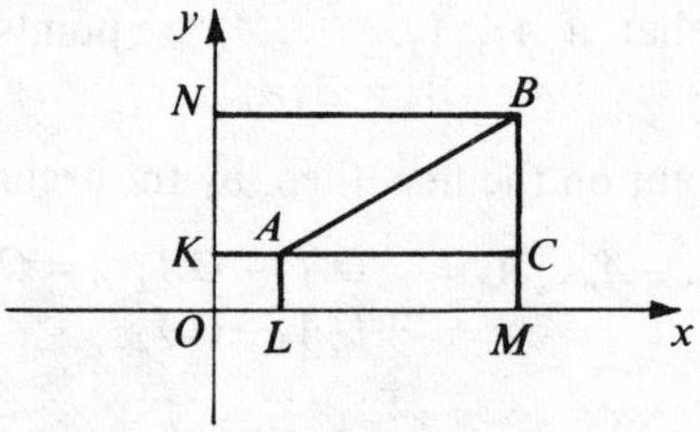

$$|AB| = \sqrt{\{(x_B - x_A)^2 + (y_B - y_A)^2\}}. \tag{2.1}$$

Proof. In the diagram shown, L and M are the projections of A and B on the x-axis, i.e. the points in which the x-axis meets the lines through A and B parallel to the y-axis, and K and N are the projections of A and B on the y-axis.

$$\begin{aligned}|AB|^2 &= |AC|^2 + |CB|^2, \text{ by Pythagoras's theorem,}\\ &= LM^2 + KN^2\\ &= (OM - OL)^2 + (ON - OK)^2\\ &= (x_B - x_A)^2 + (y_B - y_A)^2,\end{aligned}$$

and, from this, (2.1) follows.

The distance function has the following properties [We note that $|AB|$ defines a function on the set of pairs (A, B) of points of the plane.]:

(1) $|AB| \geqslant 0$ and equals 0 if and only if $B = A$.
(2) $|AB| = |BA|$.
(3) $|AC| \leqslant |AB| + |BC|$ (the **triangle inequality**).

Position ratio and the section formulae. If A, B are given points and if P is any point ($\neq B$) on the line determined by A and B, then the ratio AP/PB of the measures AP, PB of the line-segments $\overrightarrow{AP}$, $\overrightarrow{PB}$ relative to a chosen positive direction on the line is called the **position ratio** of P with respect to the ordered pair of points A, B. The ratio is independent of the choice of positive direction (and for this reason it is not necessary to indicate a positive direction) and is independent of the unit of length chosen. The ratio is clearly positive when P lies between A and B, increasing from 0 at A to 1 at the midpoint M of AB and >1 when P lies between M and B; also the ratio is negative if P lies outside the line-segment $\overrightarrow{AB}$.

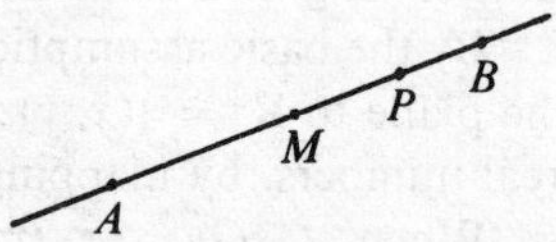

Formulae for position ratio

$$\frac{AP}{PB} = \frac{x_P - x_A}{x_B - x_P} = \frac{y_P - y_A}{y_B - y_P}.$$

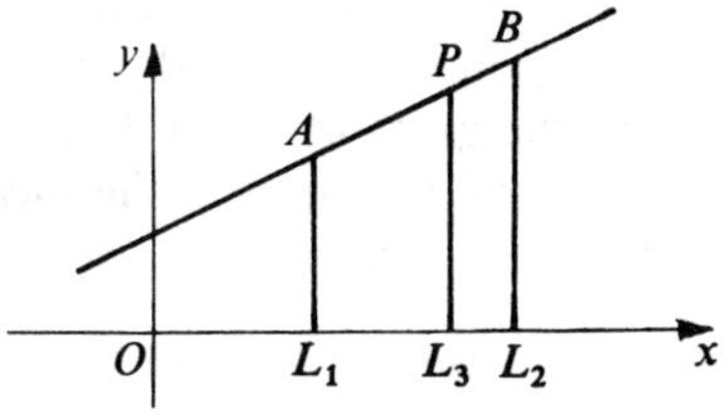

Proof. If L_1, L_2, L_3 are the projections of A, B, P on the x-axis, then

$$\frac{AP}{PB} = \frac{L_1L_3}{L_3L_2} = \frac{OL_3 - OL_1}{OL_2 - OL_3} = \frac{x_P - x_A}{x_B - x_P}.$$

Similarly, by projecting on the y-axis, we obtain the other formula for the position ratio.

The section formulae. *If* $\dfrac{AP}{PB} = \dfrac{m}{n}$, *then*

$$x_P = \frac{mx_B + nx_A}{m+n}, \quad y_P = \frac{my_B + ny_A}{m+n}. \tag{2.2}$$

Proof.

$$\frac{m}{n} = \frac{AP}{PB} = \frac{x_P - x_A}{x_B - x_P}.$$

Thus $mx_B - mx_P = nx_P - nx_A$, and so

$$x_P = \frac{mx_B + nx_A}{m+n}.$$

The expression for y_P is obtained similarly.

The **midpoint** of AB is the point $M\left(\frac{1}{2}(x_A + x_B), \frac{1}{2}(y_A + y_B)\right)$; this follows at once from (2.2) with $m = n = 1$.

Exercise. Find the coordinates of the centroid G of triangle ABC.

[Note that, if AG meets BC at A', then A' is the midpoint of BC and $AG:GA' = 2:1$.]

Gradient of a straight line (for rectangular axes). Before introducing the concept of gradient we note the following convention: If $\overrightarrow{AB}$ is a line-segment parallel to the x-axis, then AB will denote the measure of $\overrightarrow{AB}$ relative to the positive direction of the x-axis; similarly for line-segments parallel to the y-axis.

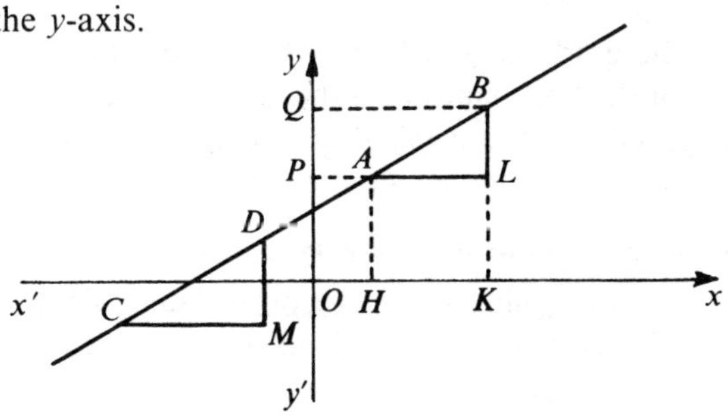

We consider first a line that is not parallel to the y-axis, and take any pair of points A, B on the line. Using the points indicated in the diagram, the **gradient** of the line is defined to be LB/AL, where LB is the measure of $\overrightarrow{LB}$ and AL the measure of $\overrightarrow{AL}$ as described in the above convention. Thus,

$$\text{gradient of given line} = \frac{LB}{AL} = \frac{PQ}{HK} = \frac{y_B - y_A}{x_B - x_A} = \frac{y_A - y_B}{x_A - x_B}. \qquad (2.3)$$

It is easily shown by similar triangles that this definition is independent of the pair of points chosen on the line; for example, for the points C, D shown,

$$\frac{y_D - y_C}{x_D - x_C} = \frac{MD}{CM} = \frac{LB}{AL} = \frac{y_B - y_A}{x_B - x_A},$$

the equality $MD/CM = LB/AL$ holding in magnitude and sign by similar triangles.

A convenient notation that is often used for gradient is

$$m_{AB} = \frac{y_B - y_A}{x_B - x_A}.$$

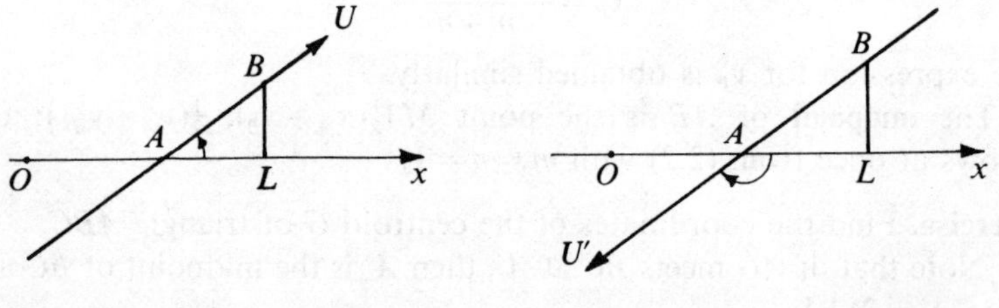

From the definition of the tangent function we have, from the above diagrams,

gradient of line determined by points A, B

$$= \frac{LB}{AL} = \tan \angle xAU = \tan \angle xAU'.$$

It follows that the gradient of a line is the tangent of any angle which either direction of the line makes with the positive direction of the x-axis.

If a line is parallel to the y-axis it has no gradient. For convenience we often say that such a line has gradient ∞.

Three important applications of gradients:

(1) Points A, B, C are collinear (i.e. lie on the same line) if and only if $m_{AB} = m_{AC}$. [This can be interpreted as "$\infty = \infty$" when the line is parallel to the y-axis.]

(2) Two distinct lines of gradient m_1, m_2 are parallel (to each other) if and only if $m_1 = m_2$.

(3) Two lines of gradients m_1, m_2 are perpendicular (to each other) if and only if $m_1 m_2 = -1$. [The only other situation in which two lines are perpendicular is that in which one line is parallel to the x-axis and the other to the y-axis.]

We shall leave details of proofs to the reader. For (3), we note that two lines are perpendicular if and only if they have, respectively, directions making angles θ and $\theta + \frac{1}{2}\pi$ with the positive direction of the x-axis. The proofs also make use of **Euclid's parallel postulate** which can be stated as: "Through each point of a plane there passes a unique line parallel to a given line in the plane."

Example 1. Show that the points $A(-1, -2)$, $B(4, -1)$, $C(5, 4)$, $D(0, 3)$ are the vertices of a rhombus (a parallelogram with perpendicular diagonals).

$$m_{AB} = \frac{1}{5} = m_{CD} \quad \text{and so } AB \text{ is parallel to } CD.$$

$$m_{BC} = \frac{5}{1} = m_{AD} \quad \text{and so } BC \text{ is parallel to } AD.$$

Thus $ABCD$ is a parallelogram. Also,

$$m_{AC} . m_{BD} = 1.(-1) = -1, \quad \text{and so } AC \text{ is perpendicular to } BD.$$

The result now follows.

Example 2. Prove that the altitudes of a triangle are concurrent. [We can assume that the triangle is not right-angled, since the result is obviously true in the right-angled case.]

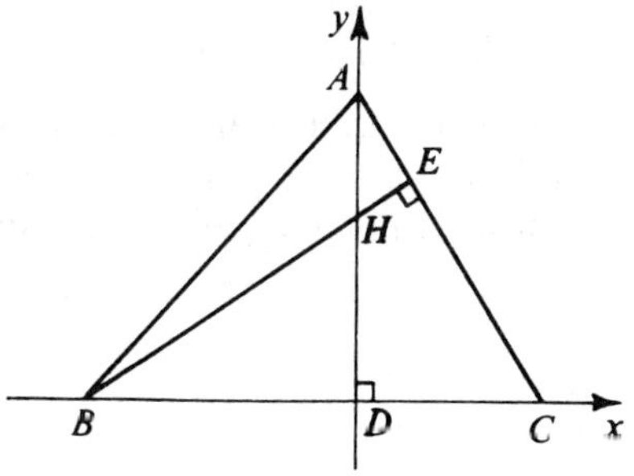

Proof. If the altitudes AD and BE meet at H we have to show that CH is perpendicular to AB.

Taking axes as indicated in the figure the points A, B, C, H will have coordinates of the form $(0, a)$, $(b, 0)$, $(c, 0)$ and $(0, h)$, respectively, with none of a, b, c, h zero.

BE perpendicular to $AC \Rightarrow m_{BE} \cdot m_{AC} = -1 \Rightarrow \left(-\frac{h}{b}\right)\left(-\frac{a}{c}\right) = -1 \Rightarrow \frac{ha}{bc} = -1.$

Now,

$$m_{CH} \cdot m_{AB} = \left(-\frac{h}{c}\right)\left(-\frac{a}{b}\right) = \frac{ha}{bc} = -1$$

and the result follows.

3. Subsets of the plane, locus

Suppose that we are given a geometrical condition involving points in the plane. The subset of the plane consisting of all the points of the plane which satisfy the condition is called the **locus** determined by the given condition. In a given coordinate system a locus is defined by restrictions involving the coordinates. For example,

(i) $\{(x, y) : x > 0, y > 0\}$ is the first quadrant;
(ii) $\{(x, y) : y = 0\}, = \{(x, 0) : x \in \mathbf{R}\}$, is the x-axis;
(iii) $\{(x, y) : x = 0\}, = \{(0, y) : y \in \mathbf{R}\}$, is the y-axis;
(iv) $\{(x, y) : y = 0, x > 0\}$ is the positive half of the x-axis;
(v) $\{P \in \text{plane} : |CP| = r$, C a fixed point of the plane and r a fixed positive real number$\}$
is the circle with centre C and radius r.

Exercise. Write down in set notation (a) the other three quadrants, (b) the negative x-axis, (c) the positive y-axis, (d) the line-segment $\overrightarrow{AB}$ where A is the point $(1, 0)$ and B the point $(3, 0)$.

If, in a given coordinate system, a locus can be expressed in the form

$$\{(x, y) : f(x, y) = 0\},$$

then the equation $f(x, y) = 0$ is called **an equation of the locus in the given coordinate system.** A point $P(x_P, y_P) \in$ the locus if and only if $f(x_P, y_P) = 0$. The equation is not uniquely determined. For example,

$$\{(x, y) : f(x, y) = 0\} = \{(x, y) : (x^2 + y^2 + 1) f(x, y) = 0\}$$

since $\{(x, y) : x^2 + y^2 + 1 = 0\} = \varnothing$.

As a particular case we note:

$$\{(x, y) : x - y = 0\} = \{(x, y) : (x - y)(x^2 + y^2) = 0\}, \text{ since}$$

$$\{(x, y) : (x - y)(x^2 + y^2) = 0\} = \{(x, y) : x - y = 0\} \cup \{(x, y) : x^2 + y^2 = 0\}$$
$$= \{(x, y) : x - y = 0\} \cup \{(0, 0)\} = \{(x, y) : x - y = 0\}.$$

Some standard simple loci in a plane.

I. Circle centre $C(a, b)$, radius r.

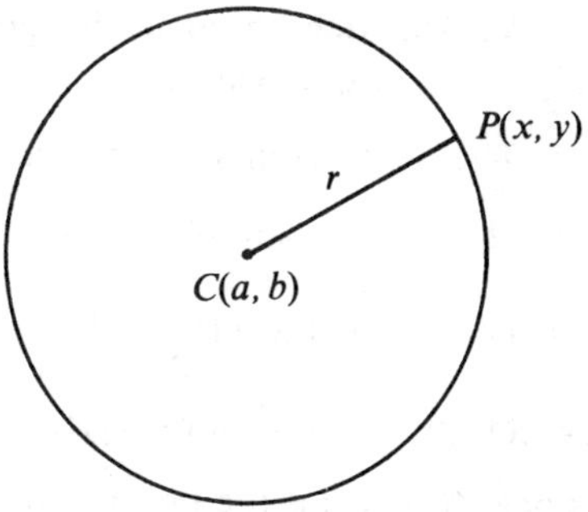

The set of points on the circle
$= \{P : |CP| = r\}$
$= \{P : |CP|^2 = r^2\}$
$= \{(x, y) : (x-a)^2+(y-b)^2 = r^2\}.$

Hence the circle has equation

$$(x-a)^2+(y-b)^2 = r^2.$$

II. *If $g^2+f^2-c \geqslant 0$, the equation $x^2+y^2+2gx+2fy+c=0$ represents a circle.*

Proof.
$$\{(x, y) : x^2+y^2+2gx+2fy+c=0\} \tag{3.1}$$
$$= \{(x, y) : (x-(-g))^2+(y-(-f))^2 = g^2+f^2-c\},$$

and so, by **I**, is the circle with centre $C(-g, -f)$ and radius $\sqrt{(g^2+f^2-c}$.

If $g^2+f^2-c=0$, the set (3.1) is $\{(-g, -f)\}$, often called a **point circle.**

If $g^2+f^2-c<0$, the set (3.1) is $\varnothing$.

III. Open circular disc, centre $C(a, b)$, radius r.

This is the subset $\{P : |CP| < r\}$, i.e.

$$\{(x, y) : (x-a)^2+(y-b)^2 < r^2\},$$

and is called the **interior** of the circle with centre C and radius r.

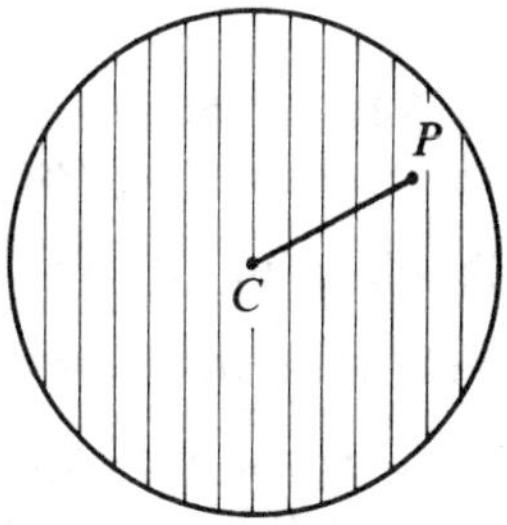

IV. The exterior of the circle, centre $C(a, b)$, radius r is

$\{P : |CP| > r\}$

$= \{(x, y) : (x-a)^2+(y-b)^2 > r^2\}.$

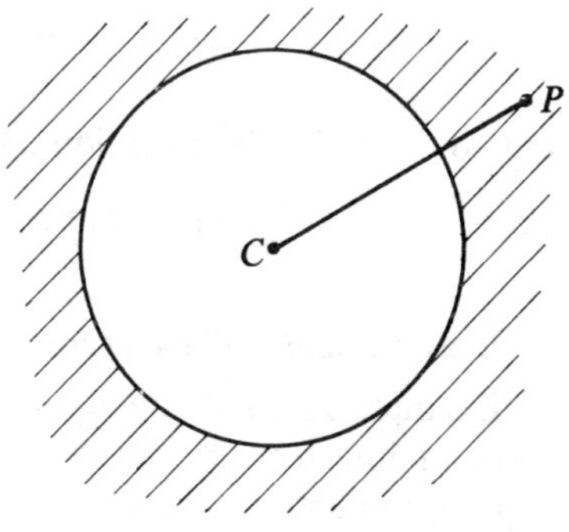

V. The line through the point $A(x_1, y_1)$ of gradient m.

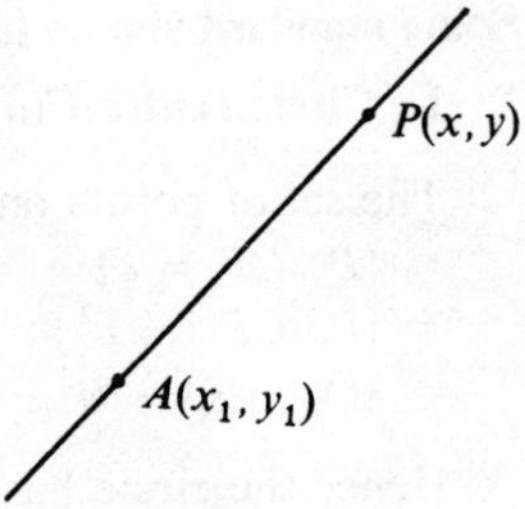

The set of points on the line

$$= \{A\} \cup \{P : m_{AP} = m\}$$

$$= \{(x_1, y_1)\} \cup \{(x, y) : \frac{y-y_1}{x-x_1} = m\}$$

$$= \{(x, y) : y-y_1 = m(x-x_1)\},$$

since $A(x_1, y_1)$ is the point in this set given by $x = x_1$.

Hence, the line has equation $y-y_1 = m(x-x_1)$.

In particular, the line through the point $A(0, c)$ with gradient m has equation $y-c = m(x-0)$, i.e. $y = mx+c$. (3.2)

VI. The line through the point $A(x_1, y_1)$ parallel to the y-axis has equation

$$x = x_1,$$

since a point $P(x, y) \in$ the line if and only if $x = x_1$.

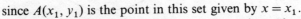

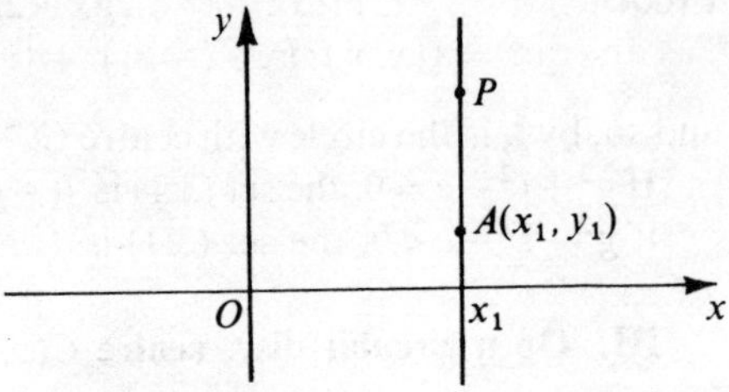

VII. *If the constants a, b are not both zero, the linear equation $ax+by+c=0$ represents a line.*

Proof. *Case* (i), $b = 0$, $a \neq 0$. In this case the equation is $ax+c=0$, and $\{(x, y) : ax+c=0\} = \{(x, y) : x = -\frac{c}{a}\}$. Thus, by **VI**, the equation represents a line parallel to the y-axis.

Case (ii), $b \neq 0$. Here

$$\{(x, y) : ax+by+c=0\} = \left\{(x, y) : y = \left(-\frac{a}{b}\right)x + \left(-\frac{c}{b}\right)\right\},$$

and so, by (3.2), the equation $ax+by+c=0$ represents the line through the point $\left(0, -\frac{c}{b}\right)$ with gradient $-\frac{a}{b}$.

4. Some examples illustrating various techniques

Example 1. Find the equation of the line which passes through the point of intersection of the lines $x+y-2=0$ and $2x-3y+1=0$ and is perpendicular to the line $x+2y=1$.

We can proceed as follows:

Let us denote the given lines in order by l_1, l_2, l_3 and let l_1, l_2 meet at the point $A(x_1, y_1)$. Consider the equation

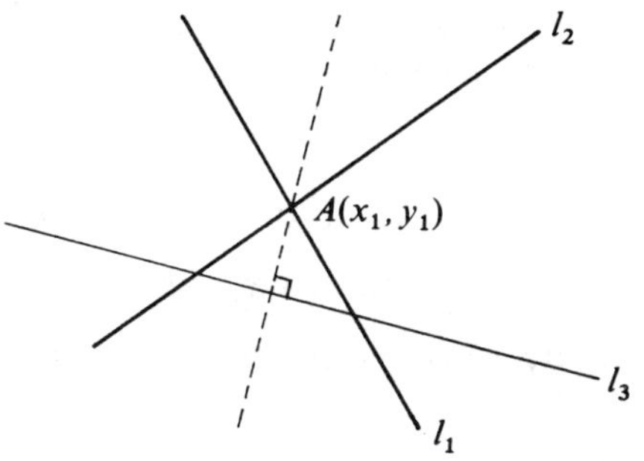

$$x+y-2+k(2x-3y+1)=0, \tag{4.1}$$

where $k \in \mathbf{R}$.

For each $k \in \mathbf{R}$, equation (4.1) represents a line. At the point A, $x_1+y_1-2=0$ and $2x_1-3y_1+1=0$ and so $(x_1+y_1-2)+k(2x_1-3y_1+1)=0$. It follows that equation (4.1) represents a line through A for each given real number k.

Conversely, each line l through A, apart from the line $2x-3y+1=0$, has an equation of the form (4.1); for, if the point $(x_2, y_2)(\neq A)$ lies on l, then l is represented by equation (4.1) with k given by $(x_2+y_2-2)+$ $+k(2x_2-3y_2+1)=0$.

To complete example 1 we have to determine k so that the line represented by (4.1) is perpendicular to l_3.

$$m_{l_3}=-\frac{1}{2},\ m_{(4.1)}=\frac{2k+1}{3k-1},$$

and so line (4.1) is perpendicular to l_3

$$\Leftrightarrow \left(-\frac{1}{2}\right)\cdot\frac{2k+1}{3k-1}=-1 \Leftrightarrow k=\frac{3}{4}.$$

From (4.1) it is now easy to check that the required line has equation $2x-y-1=0$.

Example 2. *Show that the perpendicular distance from the point $P(x_1, y_1)$ to the line $ax+by+c=0$ is*

$$\frac{|ax_1+by_1+c|}{\sqrt{(a^2+b^2)}},$$

where $|ax_1+by_1+c|$ is the absolute value of the real number ax_1+by_1+c.

We first note, by considering gradients, that any line perpendicular to the line $ax+by+c=0$ has equation of the form $bx-ay$ $=$ a constant.

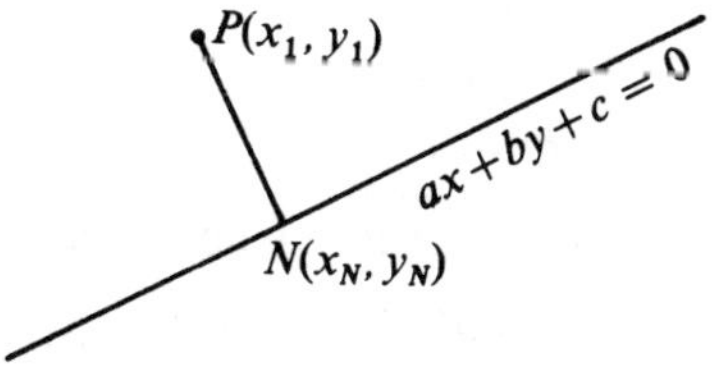

If $N(x_N, y_N)$ is the foot of the perpendicular from P to the given line, then PN has equation $bx-ay=bx_1-ay_1$, and so

$$b(x_N-x_1)-a(y_N-y_1)=0. \tag{4.2}$$

Since N lies on the given line, $ax_N+by_N+c=0$, and so

$$a(x_N-x_1)+b(y_N-y_1) = -(ax_1+by_1+c). \tag{4.3}$$

By squaring corresponding sides of (4.2) and (4.3) and adding, we have:

$$(a^2+b^2)\{(x_N-x_1)^2+(y_N-y_1)^2\} = (ax_1+by_1+c)^2.$$

Thus $$(a^2+b^2)|PN|^2 = (ax_1+by_1+c)^2,$$

and so $$|PN| = \frac{|ax_1+by_1+c|}{\sqrt{(a^2+b^2)}}.$$

Example 3. Find the equations of the tangents from the point $A(1, -2)$ to the circle $x^2+y^2-4x-2y+3=0$.

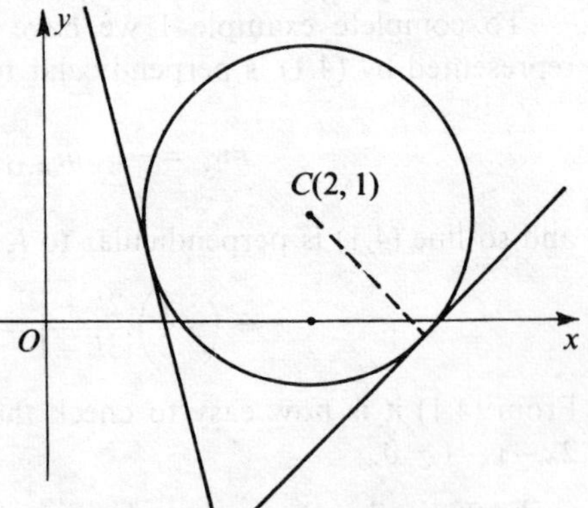

The line through the point $A(1, -2)$ with gradient m has equation

$$y-(-2)=m(x-1),$$

i.e.

$$mx-y-m-2=0. \tag{4.4}$$

The equation of the given circle is

$$(x-2)^2+(y-1)^2=2,$$

showing that the centre C has coordinates (2, 1) and the radius is $\sqrt{2}$.

Line (4.4) is a tangent from A

$\Leftrightarrow$ the perpendicular distance from C to line (4.4) equals the radius

$$\Leftrightarrow \frac{|2m-1-m-2|}{\sqrt{(m^2+1)}} = \sqrt{2}$$

$\Leftrightarrow (m-3)^2 = 2(m^2+1) \Leftrightarrow m^2+6m-7=0 \Leftrightarrow m=1$ or $m=-7$.

Thus the tangents from A have equations $x-y=3$ and $7x+y=5$.

Example 4. *If $\angle BAC$ is an angle which AC makes with AB* (i.e. *is* *obtained by rotation from AB to AC), then*

$$\tan \angle BAC = \frac{m_{AC} - m_{AB}}{1 + m_{AC} . m_{AB}}.$$

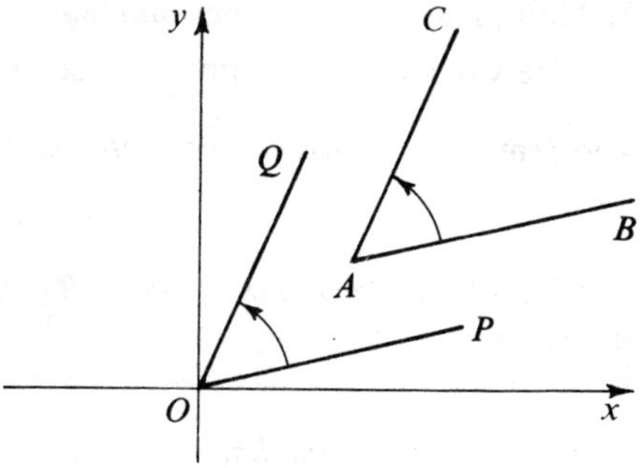

If OP, OQ are lines through O parallel to AB, AC and in the same directions, respectively, then

$$\begin{aligned}\tan \angle BAC &= \tan \angle POQ \\ &= \tan(\angle xOQ - \angle xOP) \\ &= \frac{\tan \angle xOQ - \tan \angle xOP}{1 + \tan \angle xOQ . \tan \angle xOP} \\ &= \frac{m_{AC} - m_{AB}}{1 + m_{AC} m_{AB}}, \qquad (4.5)\end{aligned}$$

by the definition of gradient and since OP, OQ are parallel to AB, AC.

Example 5. Find the equation of the reflection of the line $2x - y - 1 = 0$ in the line $x - y = 0$.

The given lines meet where

$$\begin{cases} 2x - y = 1, \\ x - y = 0, \end{cases}$$

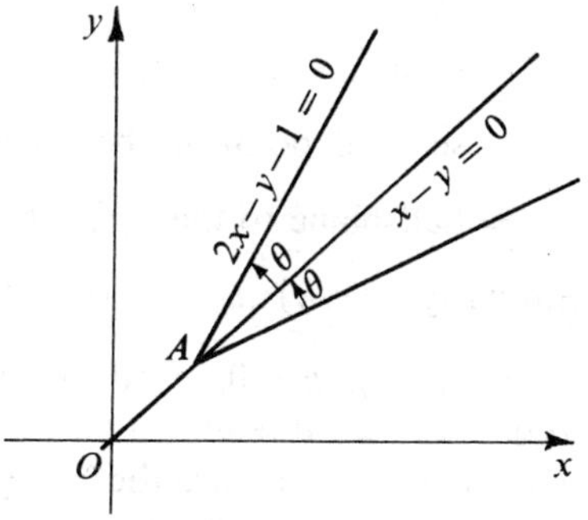

and so, on solving, at the point $A(1, 1)$.

If θ is the angle indicated between the lines $2x - y - 1 = 0$ and $x - y = 0$, then

$$\tan \theta = \frac{2 - 1}{1 + 2.1},$$

by using equation (4.5), and so

$$\tan \theta = \frac{1}{3}.$$

The line $x - y = 0$ makes an angle θ with the required line. Thus, if the required line has gradient m,

$$\frac{1}{3} = \tan \theta = \frac{1 - m}{1 + m},$$

and so $1 + m = 3 - 3m$. It follows that $m = \frac{1}{2}$ and the line has equation $y - 1 = \frac{1}{2}(x - 1)$, i.e. $x - 2y + 1 = 0$.

5. Half-planes, linear programming

The work of this section is based on the following result:

Theorem 1.3. *Given line with equation* $ax+by+c=0$, *the subset*

$$\{(x, y): ax+by+c>0\}$$

consists of all the points in the half-plane on one side of the line and the subset

$$\{(x, y): ax+by+c<0\}$$

of all the points in the half-plane on the other side.

Proof. *Case* (i), $b=0$, $a>0$.

Here the line is parallel to the y-axis and has equation

$$x=-\frac{c}{a}.$$

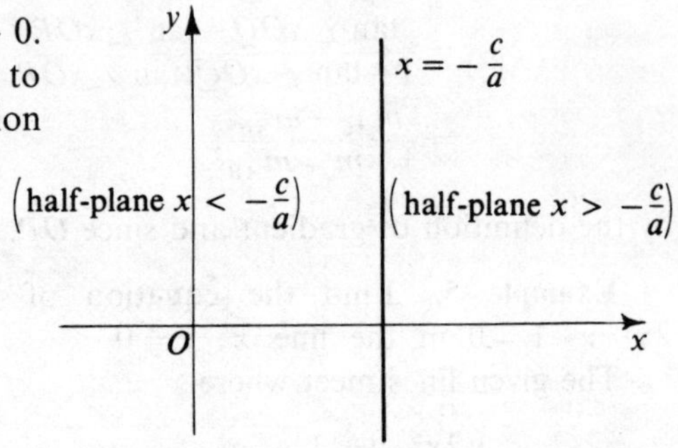

Also,

$$\{(x, y): ax+c>0\}$$

$$=\left\{(x, y): x>-\frac{c}{a}\right\},$$

since $a>0$,

$=$ set of all points in the plane with x-coordinates $>-\dfrac{c}{a}$

$=$ half-plane to the *right* of line $ax+c=0$.

Similarly, $\{(x, y): ax+c<0\}=$ half-plane to the *left* of line $ax+c=0$.

Case (ii), $b=0$, $a<0$: In this case, since $ax+c>0 \Leftrightarrow x<-(c/a)$, and $ax+c<0 \Leftrightarrow x>-(c/a)$, the subsets $\{(x, y): ax+c>0\}$ and $\{(x, y): ax+c<0\}$ are the half-planes to the left and right, respectively, of the line $ax+c=0$.

Case (iii), $b>0$:

A point (x, y) lies on the line

$$\Leftrightarrow y=-\frac{a}{b}x-\frac{c}{b}.$$

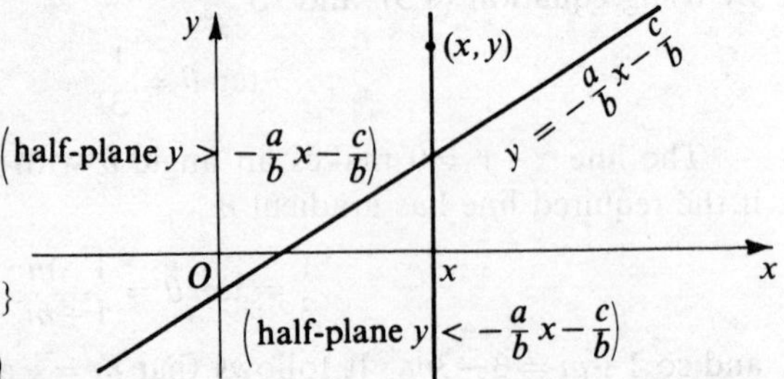

$$\{(x, y): ax+by+c>0\}$$

$$=\left\{(x, y): y>-\frac{a}{b}x-\frac{c}{b}\right\},$$

= the set of all points in the plane which, for each $x \in \mathbf{R}$, have y-coordinates $> -\frac{a}{b}x - \frac{c}{b}$

= half-plane *above* the line $y = -\frac{a}{b}x - \frac{c}{b}$, i.e. $ax+by+c = 0$.

Similarly, $\{(x, y): ax+by+c<0\}$ = half-plane *below* the line $ax+by+c = 0$.

Case (iv), $b<0$: In this case, since $ax+by+c>0 \Leftrightarrow y<-(a/b)x-(c/b)$, and $ax+by+c<0 \Leftrightarrow y>-(a/b)x-(c/b)$, the subsets $\{(x, y): ax+by+c>0\}$ and $\{(x, y): ax+by+c<0\}$ are the half-planes below and above, respectively, the line $ax+by+c = 0$.

Note. In practice, to determine the position of a half-plane relative to a given line $ax+by+c = 0$ it is enough to find the sign of the number ax_1+by_1+c, the value of $ax+by+c$ at *one* point (x_1, y_1) not on the line $ax+by+c = 0$.

For example, $\{(x, y): 2x+y-1>0\}$ is the half-plane not containing the origin (0, 0), since $2x+y-1$ has value -1 for $x = y = 0$.

Example 1. Shade the subset

$$\{(x, y): y+1>0, \quad x-2y>0, \quad 3x-y-10<0\}.$$

The subset is

$$\{(x, y): y+1>0\} \cap \{(x, y): x-2y>0\} \cap \{(x, y): 3x-y-10<0\},$$

and so is the intersection of three half-planes, its boundary consisting of parts of the lines $y+1 = 0$, $x-2y = 0$ and $3x-y-10 = 0$.

The reader should check that the region is that indicated, namely the interior of the triangle ABC.

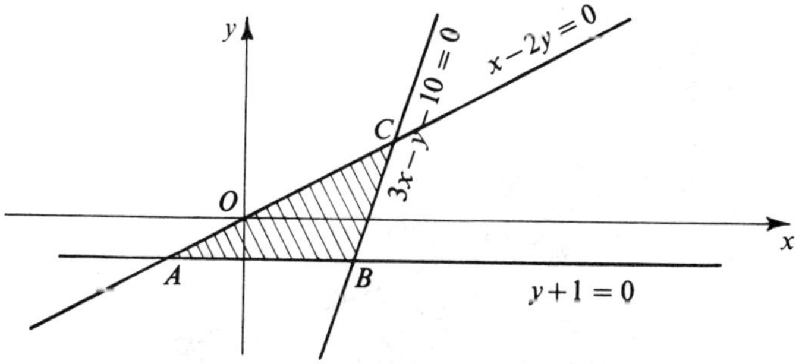

Note. The subset $\{(x, y): ax+by+c\geqslant 0\}$ is the half-plane $\{(x, y): ax+by+c>0\}$ together with its boundary $\{(x, y): ax+by+c = 0\}$, i.e. the line $ax+by+c = 0$. The subset $\{(x, y): ax+by+c \geqslant 0\}$ and also $\{(x, y): ax+by+c \leqslant 0\}$ are called **closed half-planes**; the corresponding subsets with $\geqslant$ and $\leqslant 0$ replaced by $>$ and $<$, respectively, are called **open half-planes.**

The use of open and closed half-planes has recently found an important application in **linear programming** arising in economics, cost effectiveness in industry, town planning, and so on. In most applications a large number of variables is involved and solutions require computers. We illustrate some of the ideas with a simple example.

Example 2. A furniture manufacturer makes tables and desks using timber of two types A and B. Each table requires 2 running feet of type A and 4 running feet of type B, and 3 man-hours of labour, and sells at a profit of £2. Each desk requires 5 feet of type A, 5 feet of type B, 3 man-hours of labour, and sells at a profit of £4. The manufacturer has available 1000 feet of type A, 1200 feet of type B and 810 man-hours of labour. Given that he makes x tables and y desks, write down inequalities for x, y and sketch the corresponding subset of the plane.

Determine the manufacturer's maximum possible profit.

In making the x tables and y desks,

$2x+5y$ feet of type A timber are used,
$4x+5y$ feet of type B timber are used,
$3x+3y$ man-hours are used,
£$2(x+2y)$ is made in profit.

We thus require: $x \geqslant 0$, $y \geqslant 0$, $2x+5y \leqslant 1000$, $4x+5y \leqslant 1200$, $3x+3y \leqslant 810$. Also x, y are integers, and we have to find the maximum possible value for $2(x+2y)$, and so for $x+2y$, subject to these conditions. In geometrical language we have to find the maximum possible

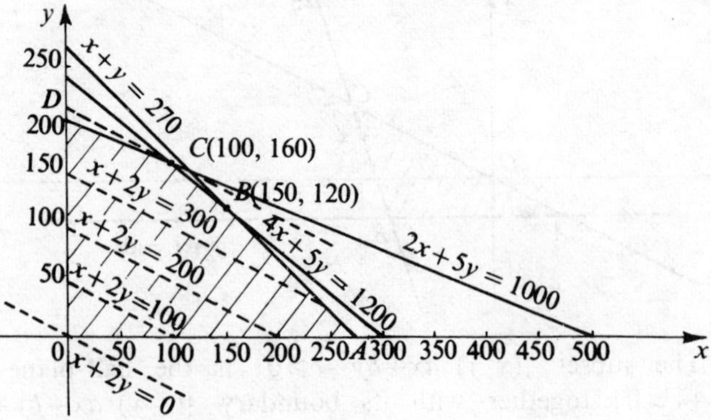

value of $x+2y$ when $(x, y) \in$ subset $\{(x, y): x \geqslant 0,\ y \geqslant 0,\ 2x+5y \leqslant 1000,\ 4x+5y \leqslant 1200,\ x+y \leqslant 270\}$, with x, y restricted to $\mathbf{Z}^+$, the set of non-negative integers.

The subset is the polygonal region $OABCD$ shown, including its boundary.

Check the diagram and the coordinates of the vertices B and C.

To maximize $x+2y$ on the closed polygonal region we have to find a point (x_1, y_1) in the region such that $x_1+2y_1 \geqslant x+2y \ \forall (x, y) \in$ region. Also, in this particular example, we have to consider only points with integer coordinates.

For each $k \in \mathbf{R}$, the equation $x+2y = k$ represents a line of gradient $-\frac{1}{2}$. Consider lines of this form which meet the region. Clearly the maximal value of $x+2y$ required will be given by the line of the form $x+2y = k$ which meets the region at a point with integer coordinates and is as far as possible from the origin. This is the line $x+2y = 420$, the line of gradient $-\frac{1}{2}$ through the vertex C of the polygon. The manufacturer should thus make 100 tables and 160 desks for a maximum profit of £840.

6. Change of coordinates

The simplest type of change of coordinate system is

Translation of axes, in which the origin O is moved to a point A, (x_1, y_1) say, with the new axes $\xi' A \xi$ and $\eta' A \eta$ (using the Greek letters ξ, η corresponding to x, y) parallel and similarly directed to $x'Ox$ and $y'Oy$.

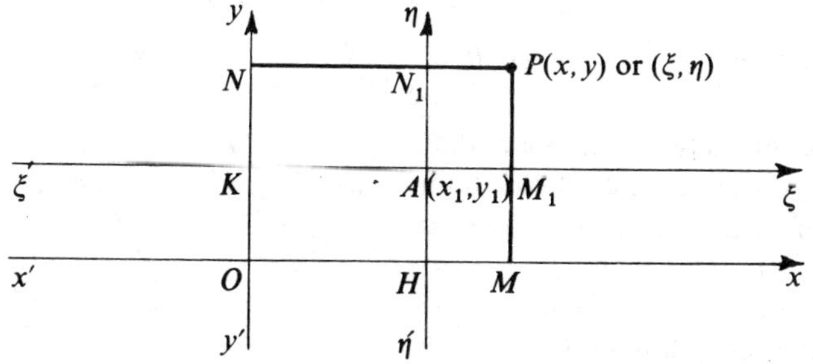

If a point P in the plane has coordinates (x, y) and (ξ, η) with respect to the two coordinate systems, then, using the points named in the diagram,

$$\xi = AM_1 = HM = OM - OH = x - x_1,$$

and (6.1)

$$\eta = AN_1 = KN = ON - OK = y - y_1.$$

On solving, we have:

$$\begin{cases} x = \xi + x_1 \\ y = \eta + y_1, \end{cases}$$

giving the old coordinates in terms of the new coordinates.

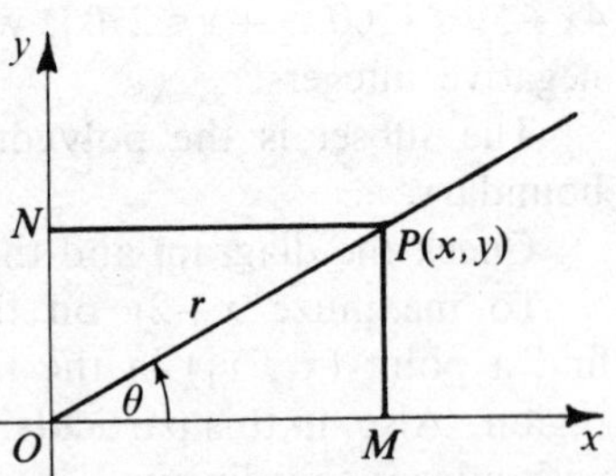

Polar coordinates. These arise in a natural way from the usual x- and y-axes. Suppose that point $P(\neq O)$ has coordinates (x, y) and that $\angle xOP$ has measure θ in radians, $0 \leqslant \theta < 2\pi$. If $r = |OP|$, then the pair of real numbers (r, θ) are called **polar coordinates** of P. Since the rotation from Ox through any angle of measure $\theta + 2k\pi$ for $k \in \mathbf{Z}$ gives rise to the same direction OP, we allow $(r, \theta + 2k\pi)$ for any $k \in \mathbf{Z}$ as polar coordinates of P. Although the origin O does not have polar coordinates, it is convenient to say that it is the point given by $r = 0$.

Since $\cos\theta = \dfrac{OM}{|OP|}$ and $\sin\theta = \dfrac{ON}{|OP|}$,

we have the following relations between polar coordinates and x, y-coordinates:

$$\cos\theta = \frac{x}{r}, \quad \sin\theta = \frac{y}{r}, \quad \text{so that} \quad x = r\cos\theta \quad \text{and} \quad y = r\sin\theta.$$

Also $$x^2 + y^2 = r^2, \quad r = \sqrt{(x^2+y^2)},$$

$$\cos\theta = \frac{x}{\sqrt{(x^2+y^2)}}, \quad \sin\theta = \frac{y}{\sqrt{(x^2+y^2)}}, \quad \tan\theta = \frac{y}{x} \ (x \neq 0).$$

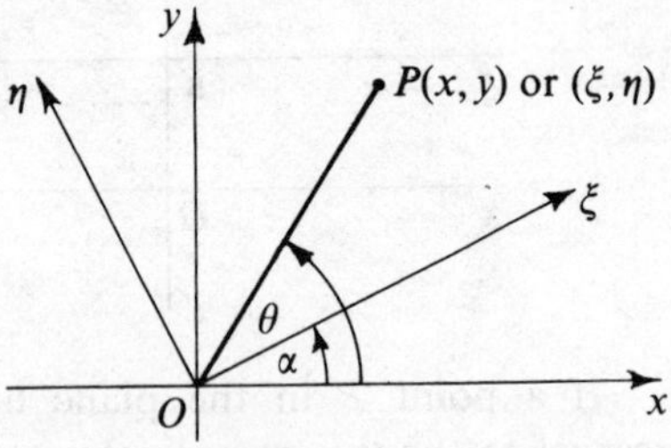

Rotation of Axes. Suppose that axes Ox, Oy are rotated through an angle of measure α (radians) to positions $O\xi$, $O\eta$; then $\angle xO\xi = \alpha$.

Suppose that a point $P(x, y)$ $(\neq O)$ has coordinates (ξ, η) with respect to the new axes $O\xi$, $O\eta$ and that $\angle xOP = \theta$; then

$$\theta = \angle xOP = \angle xO\xi + \angle \xi OP = \alpha + \angle \xi OP, \quad \text{so that} \quad \angle \xi OP = \theta - \alpha.$$

Also, $$\begin{aligned} \xi &= r\cos\angle\xi OP, \quad \text{where } r = |OP|, \\ &= r\cos(\theta - \alpha) \\ &= r(\cos\theta\cos\alpha + \sin\theta\sin\alpha) \end{aligned}$$

$$= (r\cos\theta)\cos\alpha + (r\sin\theta)\sin\alpha$$
$$= x\cos\alpha + y\sin\alpha, \tag{6.2}$$

and

$$\eta = r\sin\angle\xi OP$$
$$= r\sin(\theta-\alpha)$$
$$= r(\sin\theta\cos\alpha - \cos\theta\sin\alpha)$$
$$= -(r\cos\theta)\sin\alpha + (r\sin\theta)\cos\alpha$$
$$= -x\sin\alpha + y\cos\alpha. \tag{6.3}$$

On solving (6.2) and (6.3), we obtain:

$$\begin{cases} x = \xi\cos\alpha - \eta\sin\alpha, \\ y = \xi\sin\alpha + \eta\cos\alpha. \end{cases} \tag{6.4}$$

In matrix notation, we have:

$$\begin{bmatrix}\xi\\ \eta\end{bmatrix} = \begin{bmatrix}\cos\alpha & \sin\alpha\\ -\sin\alpha & \cos\alpha\end{bmatrix}\begin{bmatrix}x\\ y\end{bmatrix}, \quad \text{and} \quad \begin{bmatrix}x\\ y\end{bmatrix} = \begin{bmatrix}\cos\alpha & -\sin\alpha\\ \sin\alpha & \cos\alpha\end{bmatrix}\begin{bmatrix}\xi\\ \eta\end{bmatrix}.$$

Example. If the axes Ox, Oy are rotated through an angle $\frac{1}{4}\pi$ to $O\xi$, $O\eta$, find the new equation in ξ, η-coordinates of the curve with equation $xy = 1$.

With $\alpha = \frac{1}{4}\pi$, equations (6.4) become

$$\begin{cases} x = \dfrac{1}{\sqrt{2}}(\xi-\eta), \\ y = \dfrac{1}{\sqrt{2}}(\xi+\eta). \end{cases}$$

Thus equation $xy = 1$ becomes $\xi^2-\eta^2 = 2$, and this is the required equation.

7. Some geometrical transformations

The most important geometrical transformations in elementary plane geometry are those which, in terms of a given coordinate system, can be represented by linear equations. If such a transformation T maps a point $P(x, y)$ to $P'(x', y')$, then

$$\begin{cases} x' = ax+by+h_1, \\ y' = cx+dy+h_2, \end{cases} \tag{7.1}$$

where a, b, c, d, h_1, h_2 are constants.

The transformation T is a bijection from S, the set of points in the plane, to S, i.e. a one-to-one mapping of S onto S. The transformation T has an inverse T^{-1} which maps $P'(x', y')$ to $P(x, y)$ and which is represented by the linear equations obtained from (7.1) by solving for (x, y) in terms of (x', y').

In matrix notation, (7.1) can be written as:

$$Y = AX + H, \tag{7.2}$$

where $X = \begin{bmatrix} x \\ y \end{bmatrix}$, $Y = \begin{bmatrix} x' \\ y' \end{bmatrix}$, $A = \begin{bmatrix} a & b \\ c & d \end{bmatrix}$ and $H = \begin{bmatrix} h_1 \\ h_2 \end{bmatrix}$.

On solving for X in terms of Y, the matrix equation for T^{-1} is

$$X = A^{-1}Y - A^{-1}H, \tag{7.3}$$

where A^{-1} is the inverse of the matrix A, so that

$$A^{-1} = \frac{1}{(ad-bc)}\begin{bmatrix} d & -b \\ -c & a \end{bmatrix}.$$

A point $P(x, y)$ is called a **fixed point** of the transformation T if T maps P to itself. From (7.1), $P(x, y)$ is a fixed point of T if and only if

$$\begin{cases} x = ax+by+h_1, \\ y = cx+dy+h_2. \end{cases} \tag{7.4}$$

In particular, the origin $O(0, 0)$ is a fixed point of T if and only if $h_1 = h_2 = 0$, and so, if and only if T is represented by a system of **homogeneous linear equations**

$$\begin{cases} x' = ax+by, \\ y' = cx+dy, \end{cases} \tag{7.5}$$

which, in matrix notation, is

$$Y = AX. \tag{7.6}$$

If at least one of h_1, h_2 is non-zero, the system of equations (7.1) is said to be **non-homogeneous.**

We now list a few special transformations and obtain their matrix equations with respect to a given coordinate system.

I. Translation

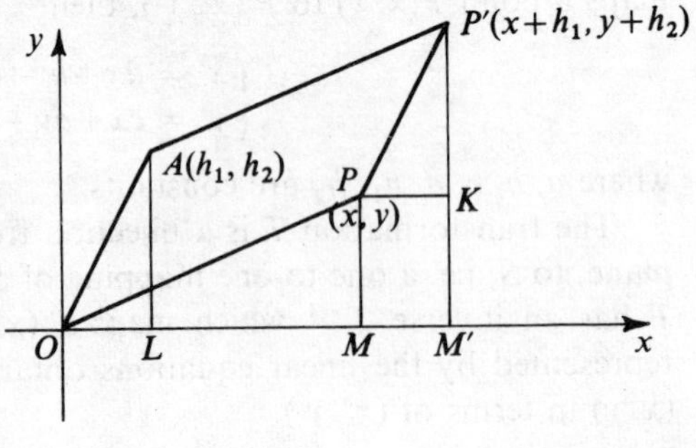

Here, if the origin O is mapped (i.e. translated) to the point $A(h_1, h_2)$, then a point $P(x, y)$ is mapped to the point $P'(x', y')$ so that the line-segments $\vec{OA}$ and $\vec{PP'}$ are directed in the same direction and have equal lengths. Thus, using similar triangles OLA and PKP' in the diagram,

$$h_1 = OL = PK = MM' = OM' - OM = x' - x.$$

Similarly, by projecting on the y-axis, we have: $h_2 = y' - y$.

It follows that the translation through the line-segment $\overrightarrow{OA}$ is represented by the equations

$$\begin{cases} x' = x + h_1, \\ y' = y + h_2, \end{cases} \tag{7.7}$$

and so by the matrix equation

$$Y = X + H = IX + H, \tag{7.8}$$

where I is the identity matrix $\begin{bmatrix} 1 & 0 \\ 0 & 1 \end{bmatrix}$.

A translation (when $A \neq O$) clearly has no fixed point.

II. Rotation about O through angle α

Here, if $P(x, y) \to P'(x', y')$, then $|OP| = |OP'|$. Also, if P has polar coordinates (r, θ), then P' has polar coordinates $(r, \theta + \alpha)$. Thus

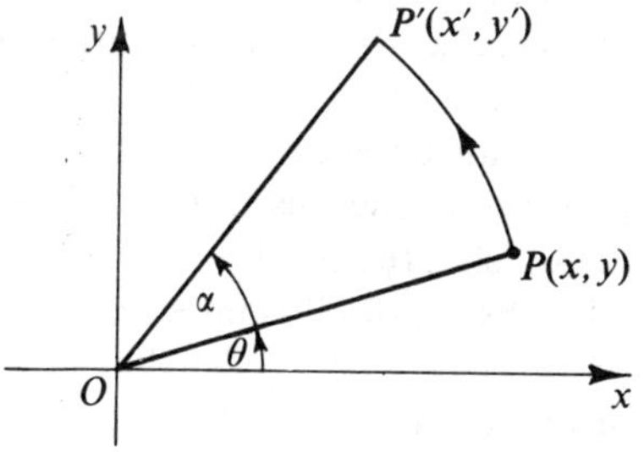

$$x' = r\cos(\theta + \alpha) = x\cos\alpha - y\sin\alpha,$$
$$y' = r\sin(\theta + \alpha) = x\sin\alpha + y\cos\alpha,$$

so that

$$\begin{bmatrix} x' \\ y' \end{bmatrix} = \begin{bmatrix} \cos\alpha & -\sin\alpha \\ \sin\alpha & \cos\alpha \end{bmatrix} \begin{bmatrix} x \\ y \end{bmatrix} \tag{7.9}$$

is the matrix equation representing the rotation.

The origin O is the only fixed point of the rotation ($\alpha \neq 2k\pi$).

III. Reflection in line OL through O making angle α with Ox

Here, if $P(x, y) \to P'(x', y')$, then $\angle LOP = -\angle LOP'$, and $r = |OP| = |OP'|$.

Now $\angle xOP' = \angle xOL + \angle LOP'$
$= \alpha - \angle LOP$
$= \alpha - (\angle xOP - \angle xOL)$
$= \alpha - (\theta - \alpha)$,
$= 2\alpha - \theta$,

where $\angle xOP = \theta$.

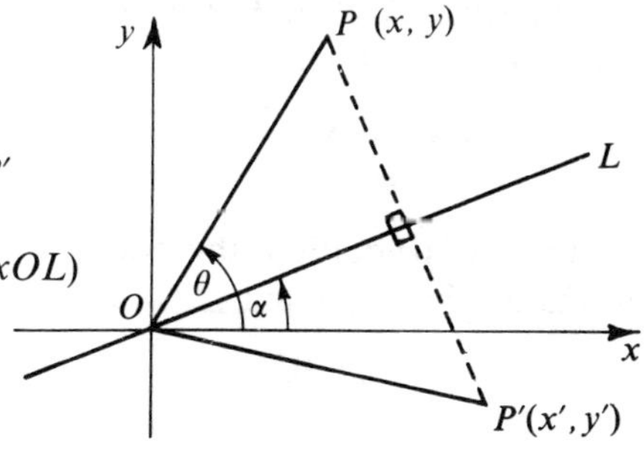

Thus, if P has polar coordinates (r, θ), then P' has polar coordinates $(r, 2\alpha-\theta)$. Hence

$$x' = r\cos(2\alpha-\theta) = r(\cos 2\alpha\cos\theta+\sin 2\alpha\sin\theta) = x\cos 2\alpha+y\sin 2\alpha,$$
$$y' = r\sin(2\alpha-\theta) = r(\sin 2\alpha\cos\theta-\cos 2\alpha\sin\theta) = x\sin 2\alpha-y\cos 2\alpha.$$

In matrix form, the equation representing the reflection is:

$$\begin{bmatrix} x' \\ y' \end{bmatrix} = \begin{bmatrix} \cos 2\alpha & \sin 2\alpha \\ \sin 2\alpha & -\cos 2\alpha \end{bmatrix}\begin{bmatrix} x \\ y \end{bmatrix}. \qquad (7.10)$$

The set of fixed points is the set of points on the line OL.

It is clear from the geometrical nature of the transformations I, II, III that, for each of them, if $P \to P'$ and $Q \to Q'$, then $|P'Q'| = |PQ|$, so that each of them *preserves distance*. Any transformation with this property is called an **isometry.** An isometry maps a figure onto a congruent figure.

An obvious question that arises is: "What condition on the matrix A ensures that the matrix equation $Y = AX+H$ of (7.2) or $Y = AX$ of (7.6) represents an isometry?"

It can be shown that the transformations represented by (7.2) and (7.6) are isometries if and only if the matrix A is an **orthogonal matrix,** i.e. satisfies the condition $A'A = I$ [Then $A' = A^{-1}$ and $AA' = AA^{-1} = I$.]. Also the set of all isometries of the plane is the set of all transformations of the types I, II, III listed and compositions of these, where composition means the usual composition of mappings.

An important plane linear transformation which is not an isometry is the **dilatation** from O involving an enlargement or scale factor $c(\neq 0$ or $\pm 1)$. Here, a point $P(\neq O)$ is mapped to a point P' such that O, P, P' are collinear and, in magnitude and sign, $OP' = cOP$. Thus, if P has coordinates (x, y), then P' has coordinates (x', y') where

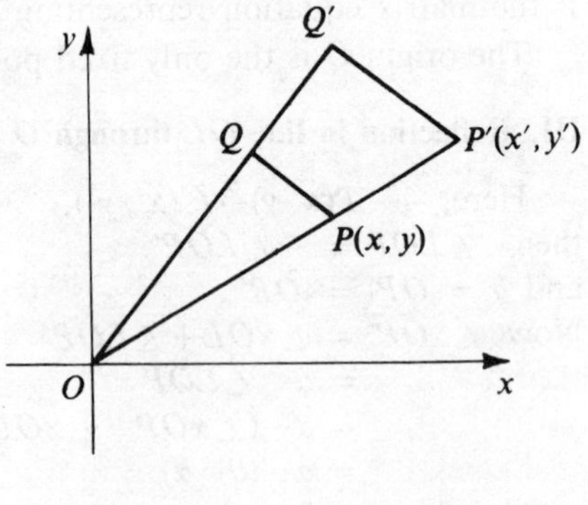

$$\begin{cases} x' = cx, \\ y' = cy. \end{cases}$$

In matrix notation, this transformation has equation

$$Y = \begin{bmatrix} c & 0 \\ 0 & c \end{bmatrix} X.$$

If also the point Q is mapped to the point Q', then $P'Q'$ is parallel to PQ and $P'Q' = cPQ$.

Example 1. Show that the equations

$$\begin{cases} x' = -x \\ y' = 2c-y \end{cases}$$

are the equations of T, the half-turn in the x, y-plane about the point $A(0, c)$. Write down equations for U, the reflection in the x-axis. Hence obtain equations for the composition $T \circ U$. Show that $T \circ U$ has a fixed point if and only if $c = 0$, and find all the fixed points when $c = 0$.

By T, $P(x, y)$ is mapped to $P'(x', y')$

$\Leftrightarrow A$ is the midpoint of $\overrightarrow{PP'}$

$\Leftrightarrow \left(\frac{1}{2}(x+x'), \frac{1}{2}(y+y')\right) = (0, c)$

$\Leftrightarrow \begin{cases} x' = -x, \\ y' = 2c-y. \end{cases}$

Thus

$$T(x, y) = (-x, 2c-y). \qquad (7.11)$$

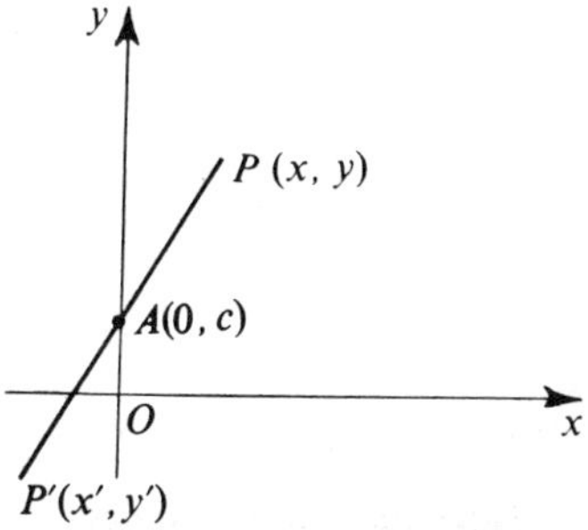

Equations for U are $x' = x$, $y' = -y$; hence

$$U(x, y) = (x, -y). \qquad (7.12)$$

Hence $(T \circ U)(x, y) = T\left(U(x, y)\right) = T(x, -y)$, using (7.12),
$= (-x, 2c+y)$, using (7.11).

It follows that equations for $T \circ U$ are

$$\begin{cases} x' = -x, \\ y' = 2c+y. \end{cases}$$

The point $P(x, y)$ is a fixed point of $T \circ U$

$$\Leftrightarrow \begin{cases} x = -x, \\ y = 2c+y, \end{cases} \Leftrightarrow \begin{cases} x = 0, \\ \text{and } c = 0. \end{cases}$$

Hence $T \circ U$ has fixed points $\Leftrightarrow c = 0$, and, when $c = 0$, the set of fixed points is the set of points satisfying $x = 0$, i.e. is the y-axis.

Example 2. R_1 is the reflection in the line $y = (1/\sqrt{3})x$ and R_2 is the reflection in the line $y = \sqrt{3}x$. By using matrices, identify the transformation $R_1 \circ R_2$.

From (7.10) with $\alpha = \frac{1}{6}\pi$ the matrix equation for R_1 is

$$Y = \begin{bmatrix} \frac{1}{2} & \frac{1}{2}\sqrt{3} \\ \frac{1}{2}\sqrt{3} & -\frac{1}{2} \end{bmatrix} X,$$

and from (7.10) with $\alpha = \frac{1}{3}\pi$ the matrix equation for R_2 is

$$Y = \begin{bmatrix} -\frac{1}{2} & \frac{1}{2}\sqrt{3} \\ \frac{1}{2}\sqrt{3} & \frac{1}{2} \end{bmatrix} X.$$

Thus
$$\begin{aligned}(R_1 \circ R_2)(X) &= R_1\left(\begin{bmatrix} -\frac{1}{2} & \frac{1}{2}\sqrt{3} \\ \frac{1}{2}\sqrt{3} & \frac{1}{2} \end{bmatrix} X\right) \\ &= \begin{bmatrix} \frac{1}{2} & \frac{1}{2}\sqrt{3} \\ \frac{1}{2}\sqrt{3} & -\frac{1}{2} \end{bmatrix}\begin{bmatrix} -\frac{1}{2} & \frac{1}{2}\sqrt{3} \\ \frac{1}{2}\sqrt{3} & \frac{1}{2} \end{bmatrix} X \\ &= \begin{bmatrix} \frac{1}{2} & \frac{1}{2}\sqrt{3} \\ -\frac{1}{2}\sqrt{3} & \frac{1}{2} \end{bmatrix} X \\ &= \begin{bmatrix} \cos(-\frac{1}{3}\pi) & -\sin(-\frac{1}{3}\pi) \\ \sin(-\frac{1}{3}\pi) & \cos(-\frac{1}{3}\pi) \end{bmatrix} X,\end{aligned}$$

and so, by (7.9), $R_1 \circ R_2$ is the rotation about O through angle $-\frac{1}{3}\pi$.

8. Introduction to conics

These important curves arose originally as plane sections of a right circular cone, but are now usually defined by a simple geometrical property called "the focus and directrix property".

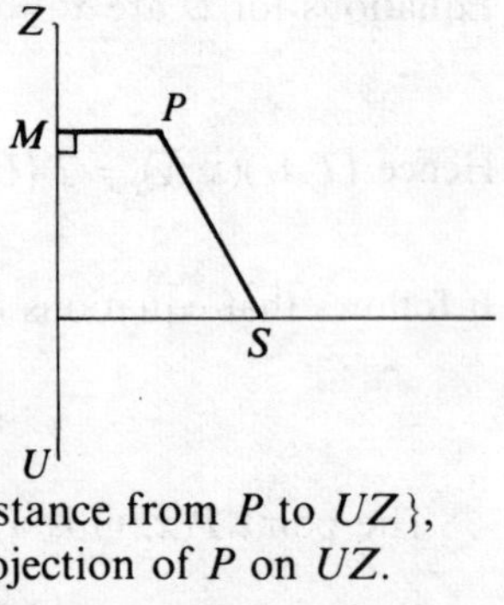

Definition. We start with a fixed point S, a fixed line UZ which does not pass through S and a fixed positive real number e.

Consider the set of points, in the plane determined by S and UZ,

$$\{P : \text{distance}|SP| = e \times \text{perpendicular distance from } P \text{ to } UZ\},$$

i.e. $\{P : |SP| = e|PM|\}$, where M is the projection of P on UZ.

Any subset of the plane which can be expressed in this form is called a **conic.** The point S is called a **focus** of the conic and the line UZ the **directrix** corresponding to the focus S. The number e is called the **eccentricity** of the conic.

The conic is called a **parabola, ellipse** or **hyperbola** respectively according as $e = 1$, $e < 1$ or $e > 1$.

Suppose that, in a given coordinate system, S has coordinates (p, q) and UZ has equation $lx + my + n = 0$. Then

$$P(x, y) \in \text{conic} \Leftrightarrow (x-p)^2+(y-q)^2 = e^2\left\{\frac{|lx+my+n|}{\sqrt{(l^2+m^2)}}\right\}^2,$$

so that this equation represents the conic. It is an equation of second degree in x, y and can be written in the form

$$ax^2+2hxy+by^2+2gx+2fy+c = 0.$$

We now make a brief systematic study of each of the three types of conic.

I. The parabola (conic with $e = 1$).

Point $P \in$ parabola $\Leftrightarrow |SP| = |MP|$.

The line XS perpendicular to UZ is called the **axis** of the parabola.

If $P \in$ parabola, then so does P' the image of P in XS. It follows that the parabola is symmetrical about the axis.

If A is the midpoint of $\overrightarrow{XS}$, then $|SA| = |AX|$ and so $A \in$ parabola. The point A is called the **vertex** of the parabola.

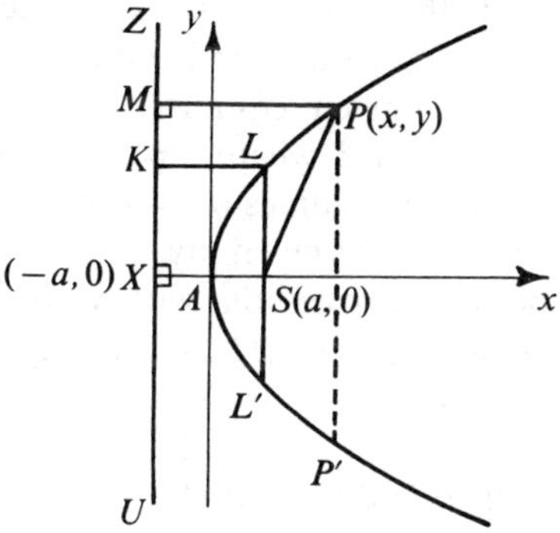

If the line through S parallel to UZ meets the parabola at L, L' then line $L'L$ is called the **latus rectum** of the parabola. By symmetry, S is the midpoint of $L'L$. The length of the latus rectum is $|L'L| = 2|SL| = 2|KL|$, where K is the projection of L on UZ,

$$= 2|XS| = 4|AS|.$$

Canonical equation of a parabola. We choose a coordinate system as follows: Take A as origin, x-axis along $\overrightarrow{AS}$ and the y-axis so that $\angle xAy = \frac{1}{2}\pi$. If $a = |AS|$, then S is the point $(a, 0)$, X is the point $(-a, 0)$ and UZ has equation $x+a = 0$.

$$\begin{aligned}\text{The parabola} &= \{P : |SP| = |MP|\}\\ &= \{P : |SP|^2 = |MP|^2\}\\ &= \{(x, y) : (x-a)^2+y^2 = (x+a)^2\}\\ &= \{(x, y) : x^2-2ax+a^2+y^2 = x^2+2ax+a^2\}\\ &= \{(x, y) : y^2 = 4ax\}.\end{aligned}$$

Thus the parabola has equation $y^2 = 4ax$ in the coordinate system chosen. This equation is called the **canonical equation** of the parabola, the word canonical implying that the equation is essentially the simplest form of equation possible.

Note. If a coordinate system is chosen with A as origin and the x-axis along $\overrightarrow{SA}$, then the parabola has equation $y^2 = 4ax$, where, in this case, $a = -|AS|$.

In drawing the parabola $y^2 = 4ax$ it is useful to note that the points $(a, \pm 2a)$ and $(4a, \pm 4a)$ lie on the parabola.

Example 1. Show that the equation $y^2 - 8x + 4y - 4 = 0$ represents a parabola with its axis parallel to the x-axis, and find the vertex, focus and directrix of the parabola.

If the x, y-axes are kept fixed, but the parabola is given a half-turn about its vertex, find the equation of the parabola in its new position.

The given equation is $y^2 + 4y + 4 = 8x + 8$, i.e. $(y+2)^2 = 8(x+1)$, i.e. $\eta^2 = 4a\xi$ where $\xi = x+1$, $\eta = y+2$ and $a = 2$. Thus, by (6.1), the equation becomes $\eta^2 = 4a\xi$ when the axes are translated to a new origin $A(-1, -2)$ given by $\xi = 0$, $\eta = 0$. It follows that the equation represents a parabola with vertex $A(-1, -2)$ and equation $\eta^2 = 8\xi$ with respect to axes $A\xi$, $A\eta$ through A parallel to Ox, Oy.

The focus S is given by $\xi(=a) = 2, \eta = 0$,
i.e. by $x+1 = 2, y+2 = 0$,

and so is the point $(1, -2)$.

The directrix has equation $\xi(=-a) = -2$, i.e. $x+1 = -2$, i.e. $x+3 = 0$.

When the parabola is given a half-turn about A, the parabola in its new position has equation $\eta^2 = -8\xi$ with respect to axes $A\xi$, $A\eta$, and so has equation $(y+2)^2 + 8(x+1) = 0$ with respect to axes Ox, Oy.

Parametric equations for the parabola $y^2 = 4ax$. We show that

$$\{(x, y) : y^2 = 4ax\} = \{(at^2, 2at) : t \in \mathbf{R}\}. \tag{8.1}$$

In the first place, since $(2at)^2 = 4a(at^2)\ \forall t \in \mathbf{R}$, it follows that the point $(at^2, 2at)$ lies on the parabola $y^2 = 4ax\ \forall\ t \in \mathbf{R}$. Conversely, if the point $(x_1, y_1) \in$ parabola so that $y_1^2 = 4ax_1$, then the point (x_1, y_1) can be expressed as $(at^2, 2at)$ with $t = y_1/2a$.

It follows that a point $(x, y) \in$ parabola if and only if $x = at^2$ and $y = 2at$ for some $t \in \mathbf{R}$. Consequently (8.1) holds; we say that the parabola $y^2 = 4ax$ has **parametric equations**

$$x = at^2, \quad y = 2at \quad (t \in \mathbf{R}). \tag{8.2}$$

Many geometrical properties of the parabola can be established by using the equations (8.2).

Example 2. (The parabolic mirror property)

The normal at a point P on a parabola bisects $\angle SPL$, where S is the focus and PL is the line through P parallel to the axis.

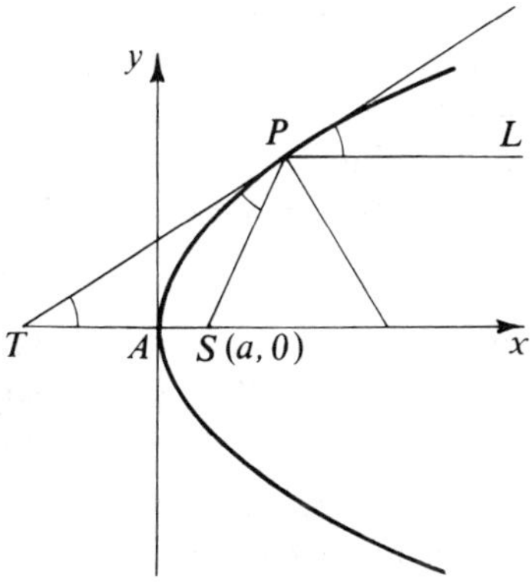

Proof. We take the equation of the parabola in canonical form $y^2 = 4ax$, and let $P(\neq$ the vertex $A)$ be a point $(at^2, 2at)$ on the parabola. If the tangent at P meets the axes at T, the required result will follow if we show that the triangle SPT is isosceles; for, then PT is one bisector of $\angle SPL$ and the normal at P, being perpendicular to the tangent PT at P, is the other bisector.

$$m_{PT} = \frac{\dot{y}}{\dot{x}} = \frac{2a}{2at} = \frac{1}{t},$$

using (8.2), [As usual $\dot{x}$ is dx/dt and $\dot{y}$ is dy/dt.], and PT has equation $ty - x = at^2$. It follows that T has coordinates $(-at^2, 0)$. Hence $|ST| = TS = a(1+t^2)$. But $|SP|^2 = (at^2-a)^2+(2at-0)^2 = a^2(t^2+1)^2$, so that $|SP| = a(1+t^2) = |ST|$, and the result follows.

This property is the basis for the parabolic reflector; if a source of light is placed at the focus S of a parabolic reflector, each ray of light from S is reflected parallel to the axis, so producing a parallel beam of light.

II. The ellipse (conic with $e<1$).

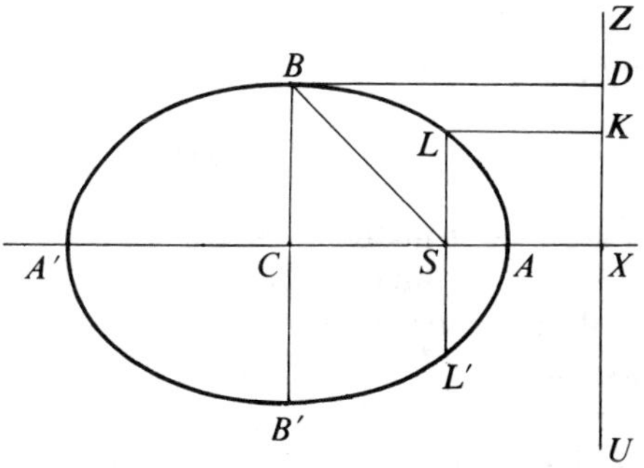

Fundamental properties. In the diagram, S is the given focus and UZ the corresponding directrix, and X is the projection of S on UZ. The points A and A' on SX such that

$$SA = eAX \quad \text{and} \quad SA' = -eA'X \tag{8.3}$$

are on the ellipse. Since these equations involving measures of line-segments are independent of choice of positive direction on SX, it is not necessary to indicate a positive direction. The points A, A' are called the **vertices** of the ellipse; $\overrightarrow{A'A}$ is called the **major axis** and its length $|A'A|$ is denoted by $2a$. The midpoint C of $\overrightarrow{A'A}$ is called the **centre** of the ellipse.

From (8.3) we deduce the following equations:

$$CS = eCA, \quad CA = eCX. \tag{8.4}$$

Proof.

$$SA = eAX \quad \text{and so} \quad CA - CS = e(CX - CA). \tag{8.5}$$

$$A'S = eA'X \quad \text{so that} \quad A'C + CS = e(A'C + CX),$$

$$\text{and so} \quad CA + CS = e(CX + CA). \tag{8.6}$$

By subtracting and adding (8.5) and (8.6), equations (8.4) follow.

From (8.4), $\quad |CS| = ae \quad$ and $\quad |CX| = a/e$.

From the definition of the ellipse, it follows that the ellipse is symmetrical about its major axis. If the line through C perpendicular to the major axis meets the ellipse at B and B', then C is the midpoint of $\overrightarrow{B'B}$; $\overrightarrow{B'B}$ is called the **minor axis** of the ellipse and its length is denoted by $2b$. We can express b in terms of a and e as follows: If D is the projection of B on UZ, then

$$|SB| = e|BD| = e|CX| = e.\frac{a}{e} = a.$$

Thus $b^2 = |CB|^2 = |SB|^2 - |CS|^2 = a^2 - (ae)^2$, and so $b^2 = a^2(1 - e^2)$.

If the line through S perpendicular to the major axis meets the ellipse at L and L', then S is the midpoint of $\overrightarrow{L'L}$; $\overrightarrow{L'L}$ is called the **latus rectum** through S. Its length is

$$|L'L| = 2|SL| = 2e|LK| \quad \text{where } K \text{ is the projection of } L \text{ on } UZ,$$

$$= 2e|SX| = 2e|CX - CS| = 2e|(1/e)CA - eCA|,$$

by (8.4). Thus $|L'L| = 2e\left(\frac{1}{e} - e\right)|CA|$ since $\frac{1}{e} > e$,

i.e. $$|L'L| = 2a(1 - e^2) = \frac{2b^2}{a}.$$

Canonical equation. We take a coordinate system with C as origin, the x-axis along $\overrightarrow{CS}$ and in that direction, and the y-axis so that $\angle xCy = \frac{1}{2}\pi$. Then S is the point $(ae, 0)$, X the point $(a/e, 0)$, $A(a, 0)$, $A'(-a, 0)$, $B(0, b)$ and $B'(0, -b)$.

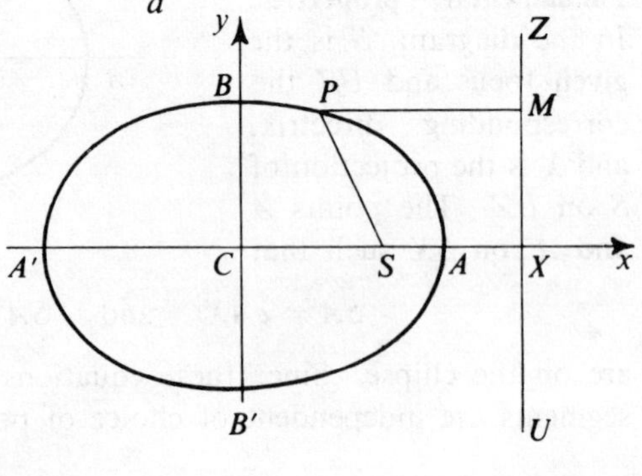

$$
\begin{aligned}
P(x, y) \in \text{ellipse} &\Leftrightarrow |SP| = e|PM| \\
&\Leftrightarrow |SP|^2 = e^2|PM|^2 \\
&\Leftrightarrow (x-ae)^2+y^2 = e^2\left(\frac{a}{e}-x\right)^2 \\
&\Leftrightarrow x^2-2aex+a^2e^2+y^2 = a^2-2aex+e^2x^2 \\
&\Leftrightarrow x^2(1-e^2)+y^2 = a^2(1-e^2) \\
&\Leftrightarrow \frac{x^2}{a^2}+\frac{y^2}{b^2} = 1, \qquad (8.7)
\end{aligned}
$$

since $b^2 = a^2(1-e^2)$. Thus the ellipse has equation (8.7) with respect to the chosen coordinate system. The equation is called the **canonical equation of the ellipse.**

Symmetry.

$P(h, k) \in$ ellipse

$$\Rightarrow \frac{h^2}{a^2}+\frac{k^2}{b^2}=1$$

$$\Rightarrow \frac{(\pm h)^2}{a^2}+\frac{(\pm k)^2}{b^2}=1.$$

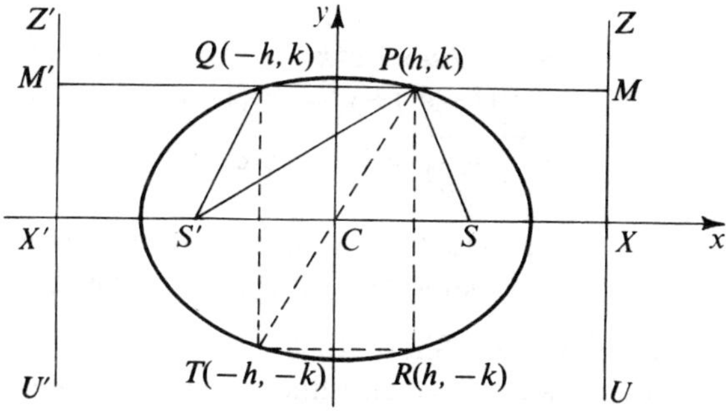

It follows that, if the point $P(h, k)$ lies on the ellipse, so do the points $Q(-h, k)$, $R(h, -k)$ and $T(-h, -k)$. Consequently the ellipse has the major and minor axes as axes of symmetry and has half-turn symmetry about C, the centre. C is the midpoint of each chord of the ellipse through C such as chord PT in the diagram.

By the symmetry in the minor axis, the parts of the ellipse on the two sides of this axis are reflections of each other. Consequently the ellipse has a **second focus** S' and corresponding directrix $U'Z'$. S' is the point $(-ae, 0)$ and $U'Z'$ is the line $x = -a/e$.

Focal distance property of the ellipse: *If P is any point on the ellipse with foci S', S and major axis of length $2a$, then*

$$|SP| + |S'P| = 2a.$$

Proof. From the diagram showing the symmetry of the ellipse, if M and M' are the projections of P on UZ and $U'Z'$, then

$$
\begin{aligned}
|SP|+|S'P| &= e|PM|+e|M'P| \\
&= e|M'M| = e|X'X| = e.2\frac{a}{e} = 2a.
\end{aligned}
$$

The following converse of the focal distance property is true.

If S', S are fixed points and a is a real number $>\frac{1}{2}|S'S|$, then the subset of the plane $\{P:|SP|+|S'P| = 2a\}$ is the ellipse with foci S', S and major axis of length $2a$.

Proof. Taking the midpoint C of $\overrightarrow{S'S}$ as origin and the x-axis along $\overrightarrow{S'S}$ and in that direction, then S has coordinates $(ae, 0)$ and $S'(-ae, 0)$, where $e = |S'S|/2a$, so that $0<e<1$.

$$\begin{aligned}
P(x, y) \in \{P:|SP|+|S'P| = 2a\}& \\
\Leftrightarrow \sqrt{\{(x-ae)^2+y^2\}}+\sqrt{\{(x+ae)^2+y^2\}} &= 2a \\
\Leftrightarrow x^2-2aex+a^2e^2+y^2+4a^2-4a\sqrt{\{(x-ae)^2+y^2\}} &= \\
&= x^2+2aex+a^2e^2+y^2 \\
\Leftrightarrow a-ex &= \sqrt{\{(x-ae)^2+y^2\}} \\
\Leftrightarrow a^2-2aex+e^2x^2 &= x^2-2aex+a^2e^2+y^2 \\
\Leftrightarrow x^2(1-e^2)+y^2 &= a^2(1-e^2) \\
\Leftrightarrow \frac{x^2}{a^2}+\frac{y^2}{b^2} = 1 \quad \text{where} \quad b^2 &= a^2(1-e^2).
\end{aligned}$$

Since the equation $x^2/a^2+y^2/b^2 = 1$ represents the ellipse with foci S', S and major axis of length $2a$, the required result follows.

Example 3. Show that the equation $x^2+3y^2-4x+24y-2 = 0$ represents an ellipse, and find its centre, eccentricity and foci.

The equation can be written in the following form

$$(x-2)^2+3(y+4)^2 = 54 \quad \text{i.e.} \quad \frac{(x-2)^2}{54}+\frac{(y+4)^2}{18} = 1,$$

$$\text{i.e.} \quad \frac{\xi^2}{54}+\frac{\eta^2}{18} = 1 \quad \text{where} \quad \xi = x-2, \eta = y+4.$$

It follows that the equation represents an ellipse whose centre is given by $\xi = 0$, $\eta = 0$ and so is the point $C(2,-4)$, and whose major and minor axes lie along the ξ, η-axes through C parallel and similarly directed to the x, y-axes.

In the standard notation for an ellipse, $a^2 = 54$ and $b^2 = 18$. But $b^2 = a^2(1-e^2)$, so that $(ae)^2 = a^2-b^2$. Thus, for this ellipse, $(ae)^2 = 54-18 = 36$, and so $ae = 6$. Since $a = 3\sqrt{6}$, it follows that the eccentricity $e = \frac{1}{3}\sqrt{6}$. The foci are given by $\xi = \pm ae$, $\eta = 0$, i.e. $x-2 = \pm 6$, $y+4 = 0$, and so are the points $(8, -4)$ and $(-4, -4)$.

Example 4. Show that, if the focus $S(ae, 0)$ is taken as origin for polar coordinates with the x-axis unchanged, then the ellipse has polar equation

$$r = \frac{l}{1+e\cos\theta},$$

where $l = b^2/a$, i.e. half the length of a latus rectum.

We have:

$$r = |SP| = e|PM|$$
$$= e\left(\frac{a}{e} - x\right)$$
$$= a - ex.$$

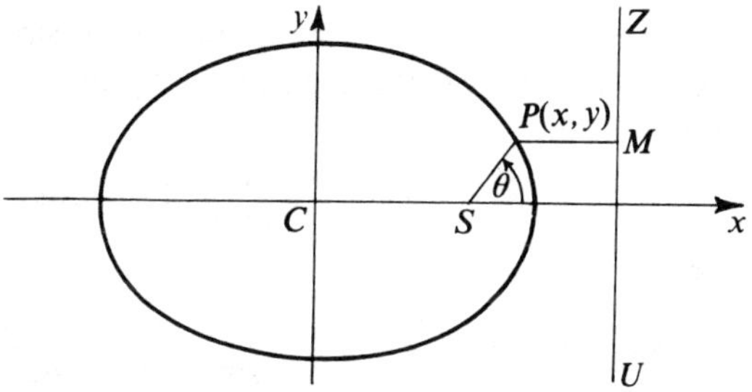

But

$$x = CS + r\cos\theta,$$
$$= ae + r\cos\theta,$$

where

$\angle xSP = \theta$.

Thus $r = a - ae^2 - er\cos\theta = b^2/a - er\cos\theta = l - er\cos\theta$,

and so $$r = l/(1+e\cos\theta).$$

Parametric equations for the ellipse $x^2/a^2 + y^2/b^2 = 1$ are

$$x = a\cos\theta, \quad y = b\sin\theta, \quad 0 \leqslant \theta < 2\pi.$$

For, the point $(a\cos\theta, b\sin\theta)$ lies on the curve since

$$\frac{1}{a^2}(a\cos\theta)^2 + \frac{1}{b^2}(b\sin\theta)^2 = \cos^2\theta + \sin^2\theta = 1.$$

Also, if the point (x_1, y_1) lies on the curve, then $|x_1| \leqslant a$ and $|y_1| \leqslant b$ and there is a unique number θ, $0 \leqslant \theta < 2\pi$, such that $\cos\theta = x_1/a$ and $\sin\theta = y_1/b$, and so $(x_1, y_1) = (a\cos\theta, b\sin\theta)$.

Example 5. Show that, if the tangent at a point P on an ellipse meets the directrix corresponding to a focus S at T, then lines SP, ST are perpendicular.

We take the equation of the ellipse in canonical form, S as point $(ae, 0)$ and $P(a\cos\theta, b\sin\theta)$.

At P, $x = a\cos\theta$ and $y = b\sin\theta$. Thus $dx/d\theta = -a\sin\theta$, and $dy/d\theta = b\cos\theta$. Consequently the tangent at P has gradient

$$\frac{dy}{dx} = \frac{dy/d\theta}{dx/d\theta} = -\frac{b\cos\theta}{a\sin\theta} \quad (\theta \neq 0 \text{ or } \pi),$$

and so the tangent has equation

$$y - b\sin\theta = -\frac{b\cos\theta}{a\sin\theta}\ (x - a\cos\theta),$$

i.e. $$b\cos\theta\, x + a\sin\theta\, y = ab,$$

i.e. $$\frac{x}{a}\cos\theta + \frac{y}{b}\sin\theta = 1. \tag{8.8}$$

Since the directrix corresponding to $S(ae, 0)$ has equation $x = a/e$, the coordinates of T are obtained by inserting $x = a/e$ in the equation (8.8); T is the point

$$\left(\frac{a}{e}, \frac{b}{\sin\theta}\left(1 - \frac{1}{e}\cos\theta\right)\right).$$

Hence

$$m_{SP}.m_{ST} = \frac{b\sin\theta}{a\cos\theta - ae}\cdot\frac{b(1-(1/e)\cos\theta)}{\sin\theta((a/e) - ae)}$$
$$= -\frac{b^2(e-\cos\theta)}{a^2(e-\cos\theta)(1-e^2)} = -1 \quad \text{since } b^2 = a^2(1-e^2).$$

It follows that SP and ST are perpendicular.

III. The hyperbola (conic with $e > 1$).

Fundamental properties.

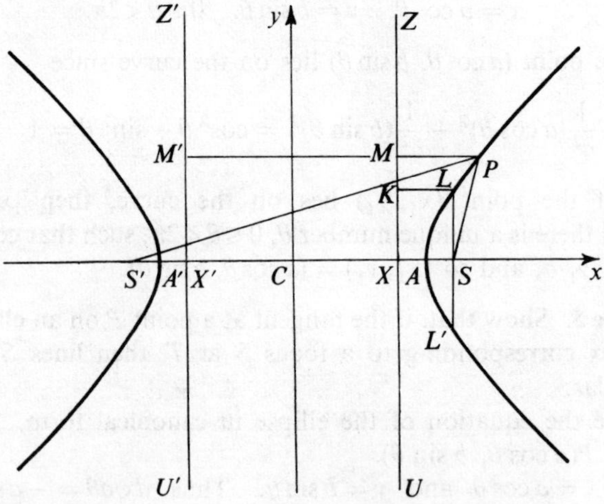

In the diagram, S is the given focus and UZ the corresponding directrix, and X is the projection of S on UZ. The points A and A' on SX such that

$$SA = eAX \quad \text{and} \quad A'S = eA'X \tag{8.9}$$

lie on the hyperbola. The points A, A' are called the **vertices** of the hyperbola and $\overrightarrow{A'A}$ is called the **transverse axis**; C, the midpoint of $\overrightarrow{A'A}$, is called the **centre.**

With the same argument as that used for the ellipse we can show, from (8.9), that

$$CS = eCA, \quad CX = (1/e)CA \quad \text{so that} \quad |CS| = ae, \quad |CX| = a/e,$$

where $|CA| = a$.

The latus rectum through S is $\overrightarrow{L'L}$, as shown in the diagram; its length is

$$\begin{aligned}|L'L| &= 2|SL| = 2e|KL| = 2e|XS| = 2e|CS-CX| = 2e(e-(1/e))|CA|\\ &= 2a(e^2-1) = 2(b^2/a),\end{aligned}$$

where b is the positive number defined by the equation $b^2 = a^2(e^2-1)$.

Canonical equation. As for the ellipse we take a coordinate system with C as origin, the x-axis along $\overrightarrow{CS}$ and in that direction, and the y-axis so that $\angle xCy = \frac{1}{2}\pi$. Then S is the point $(ae, 0)$, X the point $(a/e, 0)$, $A(a, 0)$ and $A'(-a, 0)$.

$$\begin{aligned}P(x, y) \in \text{hyperbola} &\Leftrightarrow |SP| = e|PM|\\ &\Leftrightarrow (x-ae)^2+y^2 = e^2(x-(a/e))^2\\ &\Leftrightarrow x^2(e^2-1)-y^2 = a^2(e^2-1)\\ &\Leftrightarrow \frac{x^2}{a^2}-\frac{y^2}{b^2} = 1, \qquad (8.10)\end{aligned}$$

since $b^2 = a^2(e^2-1)$. Thus the hyperbola has equation (8.10) with respect to the chosen coordinate system; this equation is called the **canonical equation of the hyperbola.**

The hyperbola does not meet the y-axis, but it is, for some purposes, convenient to introduce the points $B'(0, -b)$ and $B(0, b)$ on the y-axis and to call $\overrightarrow{B'B}$ the **conjugate axis** of the hyperbola. The hyperbola with equation $x^2/a^2-y^2/b^2 = -1$ is called the **conjugate hyperbola.**

Symmetry. As for the ellipse we deduce from equation (8.10) that a hyperbola has its transverse axis and its conjugate axis as axes of symmetry and it has half-turn symmetry about its centre C. By the symmetry in the conjugate axis, the parts of the hyperbola on the two sides of this axis are reflections of each other. Consequently the hyperbola has a **second focus** S' and corresponding directrix $U'Z'$. S' is the point $(-ae, 0)$ and $U'Z'$ is the line $x = -a/e$. The two separate congruent halves of the hyperbola are called the two **branches** of the hyperbola.

Focal distance property of a hyperbola. *If P is any point on that branch of the hyperbola with foci S, S' and transverse axis of length $2a$, which is nearer to S, then*

$$|S'P|-|SP| = 2a.$$

Conversely, if S', S are fixed points and a is a real number $<\frac{1}{2}|S'S|$, then the subset of the plane $\{P : |S'P|-|SP| = 2a\}$ is that branch which is nearer to S of the hyperbola with foci S, S' and transverse axis of length $2a$.

Exercise. Write out proofs of these results similar to the proofs of the corresponding results for the ellipse.

Asymptotes of a hyperbola. We show that the hyperbola

$$\frac{x^2}{a^2}-\frac{y^2}{b^2} = 1 \tag{8.10}$$

has two asymptotes, given by the equation $x^2/a^2-y^2/b^2 = 0$ and so by the pair of equations $x/a-y/b = 0$ and $x/a+y/b = 0$, i.e. by $y = (b/a)x$ and $y = -(b/a)x$. The meaning of this statement will be clarified during the discussion.

From (8.10), $y = \pm b/a\sqrt{(x^2-a^2)}$, and the part of the hyperbola in the first quadrant is

$$\{(x, y) : y = \frac{b}{a}\sqrt{(x^2-a^2)}, x>a\}. \tag{8.11}$$

It is clear that the curve exists only where $x^2-a^2 \geqslant 0$, and so, if $x>0$, only for $x \geqslant a$; $x = a$ gives the point $A(a, 0)$ on the x-axis.

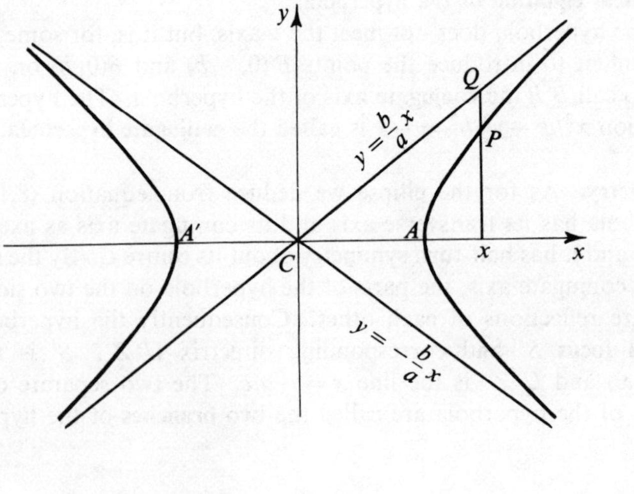

We now take $x>a$ and denote by P, Q the point in which the line through the point $(x, 0)$ parallel to the y-axis meets the part (8.11) and the line $y=(b/a)x$.

Then

$$y_Q - y_P = \frac{b}{a}x - \frac{b}{a}\sqrt{(x^2-a^2)}$$
$$= \frac{b}{a}\cdot\frac{x^2-(x^2-a^2)}{x+\sqrt{(x^2-a^2)}} = \frac{ab}{x+\sqrt{(x^2-a^2)}}.$$

It follows that, $\forall\, x>a$, $y_Q-y_P>0$ and so P is below Q; also as $x\to\infty$, y_Q-y_P decreases steadily and $\to 0$. Hence the hyperbola has the line $y=(b/a)x$ as an asymptote with approach in the first quadrant as indicated in the diagram.

Symmetry about the x-axis shows that the line $y=-(b/a)x$ is also an asymptote, approached from above in the fourth quadrant.

Symmetry about the y-axis gives the approaches to these asymptotes in the second and third quadrants.

Rectangular hyperbola

A hyperbola whose asymptotes are perpendicular to each other is called a **rectangular hyperbola.** Since the gradients of the asymptotes of the hyperbola $(x^2/a^2)-(y^2/b^2)=1$ are $\pm b/a$, a hyperbola is rectangular $\Leftrightarrow -b^2/a^2=-1 \Leftrightarrow b^2=a^2 \Leftrightarrow b=a$, since $a>0$ and $b>0$, $\Leftrightarrow a^2(e^2-1) = a^2 \Leftrightarrow e^2=2$. Thus a hyperbola is rectangular $\Leftrightarrow$ its eccentricity is $\sqrt{2}$.

Note. For the ellipse $(x^2/a^2)+(y^2/b^2)=1$, we have $b\leqslant a$, but, for the hyperbola $(x^2/a^2)-(y^2/b^2)=1$, the only restriction on b is $b>0$.

Example 6. Show that the equation $x^2-4y^2-6x-8y-15=0$ represents a hyperbola and find the coordinates of its centre and foci and the equations of its asymptotes.

The equation can be written in the form

$$(x-3)^2-4(y+1)^2=20 \quad \text{i.e.} \quad \frac{\xi^2}{20}-\frac{\eta^2}{5}=1,$$

where $\xi=x-3$, $\eta=y+1$. Thus, by translating the axes to the point $\xi=\eta=0$, i.e. $C(3, -1)$, as new origin, the equation is in the form of a canonical equation for a hyperbola. Hence the equation represents a hyperbola with centre $C(3, -1)$.

In the standard notation, $a^2=20$ and $b^2=5$; but $b^2=a^2(e^2-1)$, so that $(ae)^2=a^2+b^2$. Hence, for this hyperbola, $(ae)^2=25$ and $ae=5$.

The foci are the points given by $\xi = \pm ae$, $\eta = 0$, i.e. by $x-3 = \pm 5$, $y+1 = 0$; thus the foci are the points $(8, -1)$ and $(-2, -1)$.

The asymptotes of the hyperbola have equations $(\xi/2\sqrt{5}) \pm (\eta/\sqrt{5}) = 0$, i.e. $x-3 \pm (2y+2) = 0$, and so are the lines $x+2y-1 = 0$ and $x-2y-5 = 0$.

Exercise (Parametric equations). Show that the hyperbola $(x^2/a^2)-(y^2/b^2) = 1$ has parametric equations $x = a \sec\theta$, $y = b \tan\theta$, where $\theta \in [0, 2\pi) - \{\frac{1}{2}\pi, \frac{3}{2}\pi\}$, and obtain the equation of the tangent to the hyperbola at the point $P(\theta)$, $(\theta \neq 0, \pi)$.

EXERCISE 1

1. The centroid of a set of n points $A_1, A_2, \ldots, A_n$ on a directed line is defined to be the point G on the line such that

$$GA_1 + GA_2 + \ldots + GA_n = 0.$$

If O is any point on the line, show that

(i) $OG = 1/n(OA_1 + OA_2 + \ldots + OA_n)$,

(ii) $GA_1^2 + GA_2^2 + \ldots + GA_n^2 = OA_1^2 + OA_2^2 + \ldots + OA_n^2 - nOG^2$.

2. The projections of the points $C(4, 12)$ and $P(x, y)$ on the x-axis are A and M, respectively, the projections of C and P on the y-axis are B and N, respectively, and O is the origin. Show that the set

$$\{P : OM.MA + ON.NB = |OP|^2\}$$

is the circle on OD as diameter, where D is the midpoint of OC.

3. Show that, if A is the point $(-8, 4)$ and B $(-2, 1)$, the set

$$\{P : |AP| = 2|BP|\}$$

is a circle with the origin as centre.

4. Find the equation of the circle which passes through the points $A(4, 3)$, $B(1, 4)$, $C(5, -4)$.

5. From a point $A(h, 0)$ on the x-axis perpendiculars are drawn to the lines $x-y+1 = 0$ and $x+2y-2 = 0$ meeting them at B and C. Find the values of h for which the line BC passes through the point $(-1, 3)$.

6. A is the point of intersection of the lines with equations $12x+3y-4 = 0$ and $7x-5y+3 = 0$. Find the equation of

(i) the line joining A to the point $(8, 2)$,

(ii) the line through A parallel to the line $x+y = 0$.

7. Prove that if $u(x, y) = 0$, $v(x, y) = 0$, $u(x, y) = a$, $v(x, y) = b$ are the equations of the sides of a parallelogram ($u(x, y)$, $v(x, y)$ being linear expressions in x and y, and a, b being constants), then the equations of the diagonals are $bu-av = 0$ and $bu+av = ab$.

8. Find the equations of the two tangents from the point $(-2, 4)$ to the circle $x^2+y^2-6x+12y+20 = 0$.

9. Verify that the circle C with equation $x^2+y^2-8x+6y-11=0$ is the inscribed circle of the triangle ABC whose sides BC, CA, AB have equations $x=10$, $4x+3y+23=0$, $7x-24y+50=0$, respectively.

10. If M is the point (4, 0) and $N(0, 3)$, find the coordinates of the point P on the line l with equation $3x-y=7$ for which l is a bisector of angle MPN.

11. If B and C are the points (1, 2) and (−1, 1), respectively, find $\tan\angle BOC$, where O is the origin. Find the point $A(0, a)$ on the y-axis for which O, B, C, A are concyclic points.

12. If an equilateral triangle has sides of gradients m_1, m_2, m_3, show that $m_1m_2+m_2m_3+m_3m_1=-3$.

13. Indicate in a diagram in the plane the region

$$\{(x, y):(x-y)(x-2y)<0\},$$

and hence describe the region

$$\{(x, y):(x-y)(x-2y)(2x+y+4)>0\}.$$

14. During a certain period, the Ruritanian Electricity Generating Board has £100 million to spend on building new power stations, each of which may be a nuclear power station costing £4 million or a coal-fired power station costing £2 million. For each nuclear station built the Board will require 2 engineers and 2 physicists, and for each coal-fired station built they will require 4 engineers and 3 physicists. If the available personnel consists of 90 engineers and 70 physicists, find the maximum number of power stations that the Board can build.

15. Find the greatest and least values attained by the function $3x+4y$ of two integers x and y subject to the conditions

$$x+y-7\leqslant 0, \quad x-3y+5\geqslant 0, \quad x+2y-6>0.$$

16. In an operation it is required to transport at least 800 personnel, and at least 120,000 kg of equipment and 72,000 kg of fuel. Two types of aircraft are available, the operating costs of the first being 10% higher than those of the second. The first type is fitted out to take 40 personnel, 4000 kg of equipment and 1000 kg of fuel; the second type to take 10 personnel, 3000 kg of equipment and 6000 kg of fuel. If the operation is carried out using x flights of the first type of aircraft and y flights of the second type, determine x and y so as to minimise the cost.

How many additional personnel, or how much additional equipment or fuel beyond the minimal quantities required could be carried without extra transport costs?

17. Let $S=\{(x, y):x\geqslant 0,\ x^2+y^2\leqslant 50,\ x+y-8\leqslant 0,\ 2x+y-5\geqslant 0\}$.

Find the maximum and minimum values of $x+2y$ for points in the region S.

18. A company operates two mines, each producing low-, medium-, and high-grade coal. The daily production of each of the mines is given by the table:

Daily production (tons)

	Low	Medium	High
Mine 1	100	400	100
Mine 2	100	100	300

The company is committed to providing its customers with 4000 tons of low-grade coal, 6400 tons of medium-grade coal and 6000 tons of high-grade coal. If it costs £500 per day to operate Mine 1 and £400 per day to operate Mine 2, how many days should each mine be operated in order to meet the customers' requirements as cheaply as possible? Of which grade of coal will there be a surplus?

19. A small village factory produces items of two types, A and B. Of the three craftsmen working in the factory the first two each work a 40 hour week, while the third (who also owns the factory) works a 52 hour week. To produce a single item of type A, Craftsman 1 must work for 1 hour, while Craftsmen 2 and 3 must each work for 2 hours. To produce a single item of type B, the craftsmen must work for $2\frac{1}{2}$ hours, 1 hour and 3 hours respectively.

If the profits on items of types A and B are £3 and £4 respectively, how many items of each type should the factory produce in order to maximize the weekly profit?

20. Find the equations in terms of polar coordinates for the following curves (i) $x^2+y^2=1$, (ii) $x^2+y^2-2ax=0$, a constant, (iii) $x^2+y^2-2by=0$, b constant, (iv) $x=2$.

21. P is the point with polar coordinates (1, 0). Find polar coordinates for the point Q in the first quadrant such that PQ is perpendicular to OP and has length 1. The point R is such that QR is perpendicular to OQ and has length 1, $\angle QOR$ being positive. If R has polar coordinates (r, θ) with $r>0$, find r and show that $\tan\theta = 3+2\sqrt{2}$.

22. If the x, y-axis are rotated through angle $\frac{1}{2}\pi$ to positions 0ξ, 0η, find the equation of the parabola $y^2=4ax$ and of the ellipse $x^2/a^2+y^2/b^2=1$ with respect to these axes.

Find also the equations of these curves with respect to the axes Ax', Ay' obtained by translating the x, y-axes to the point $A(1, 2)$ as a new origin.

23. Show that the curve $-x^2+4xy+2y^2=6$ has equation $3\xi^2-2\eta^2=6$ in the coordinate system determined by the matrix equation

$$\begin{bmatrix} x \\ y \end{bmatrix} = \frac{1}{\sqrt{5}}\begin{bmatrix} 1 & -2 \\ 2 & 1 \end{bmatrix}\begin{bmatrix} \xi \\ \eta \end{bmatrix}.$$

24. Describe the transformations S, T, U, leaving the origin O fixed, which are defined, respectively, by the matrices

$$A=\begin{bmatrix} 1 & 0 \\ 0 & -1 \end{bmatrix},\quad B=\begin{bmatrix} 0 & 1 \\ 1 & 0 \end{bmatrix},\quad C=\frac{1}{\sqrt{2}}\begin{bmatrix} 1 & -1 \\ 1 & 1 \end{bmatrix}.$$

Find the matrices of the transformations $S\circ T$, $S\circ U$, $T\circ U$, $T\circ S$, $U\circ S$ and $U\circ T$, and describe each of these transformations.

25. (i) Show that, if R_1, R_2 are rotations about O, then $R_1\circ R_2 = R_2\circ R_1$. (ii) Determine whether the corresponding result for reflections in lines through O is also true.

26. Write down equations representing the transformation E, where E is the dilatation from the point $A(1, 0)$ with scale factor 2. If R is the reflection in the line $y=\sqrt{3}x$, find equations for the transformation $R\circ E$, and find the unique fixed point of $R\circ E$.

27. Find an isometric transformation which maps triangle ABC to triangle $A'B'C'$, where A is the point (2, 1), $B(2, -3)$, $C(5, -3)$, $A'(10, 4)$, $B'(14, 4)$ and $C'(14, 1)$.

28. By using equations (7.2) and (7.6) show that a linear transformation of the plane can be expressed in the form $T \circ R$, where R is a linear transformation which leaves the origin O fixed, and T is a translation.

29. Find a dilatation from O which maps the parabola $y = ax^2$ to the parabola $y = x^2$.

Under what conditions on a, b, a_1 and b_1 is there a dilatation from O which maps the ellipse $x^2/a^2 + y^2/b^2 = 1$ onto the ellipse $x^2/a_1^2 + y^2/b_1^2 = 1$.

30. If z, z' are the complex numbers $x + iy$ and $x' + iy'$, respectively, and if $h = h_1 + ih_2$ is a fixed complex number, show that

(i) $z' = z + h$ represents a translation;
(ii) $z' = z(\cos\alpha + i\sin\alpha)$ represents the rotation about the origin O through angle α;
(iii) $z' = \bar{z}$, the complex conjugate of z, represents the reflection in the x-axis;
(iv) $z' = az$, where $a \in \mathbf{R}$, represents a dilatation from O of scale factor a.

Write down an equation for the inverse of each of these transformations.

31. What is the image of the ellipse $x^2/a^2 + y^2/b^2 = 1$, where $a > 0$ and $b > 0$, under the transformation defined by the equations $x' = x/a$ and $y' = y/b$?

Show also that, by this transformation, a rectangular area with edges parallel to the x- and y-axes of lengths a/n and b/n, respectively, is mapped to a square of area $1/n^2$.

Deduce a plausible reason for the fact that the area enclosed by the ellipse has measure πab.

32. Show that each of the following equations represents a parabola and find the focus, vertex, directrix and axis of each parabola:

(i) $y^2 - 8x + 2y + 9 = 0$,
(ii) $y^2 + 2x - 4y + 7 = 0$.

33. Prove that, if the tangent at a point P on a parabola meets the directrix in Z and the tangent at the vertex in Y, then SY is perpendicular to PZ and SZ is perpendicular to SP, S being the focus.

[*Hint.* Use the parametric equations $x = at^2$, $y = 2at$ for the parabola $y^2 = 4ax$.]

34. Show that the equations

$$y^2 = 4a(a + x), \quad y^2 = 4a(a - x) \quad (a > 0)$$

represent congruent parabolas having the same focus.

35. Prove that the tangents at the points $P(t_1)$ and $Q(t_2)$ on the parabola $x = at^2$, $y = 2at$ intersect at the point $\big(at_1t_2, a(t_1 + t_2)\big)$.

Show that the orthocentre of the triangle formed by any three tangents to a parabola lies on the directrix of the parabola.

36. Show that the equation $3x^2 + 4y^2 + 24x - 8y + 4 = 0$ represents an ellipse, and find its eccentricity e and the coordinates of its foci.

37. Find, for the ellipse defined by each of the following sets of data, in the usual notation, the eccentricity e and the equation of the ellipse:

(i) $A(11, 0)$, $S(5, 0)$, latus rectum of length 15;
(ii) $S(1, 2)$, $B(-2, 6)$, major axis parallel to the x-axis;
(iii) $S'(-8, 4)$, $S(4, 4)$, latus rectum of length 7.

38. If $a>b>0$, show that the equations

$$\frac{x^2}{a^2}+\frac{y^2}{b^2}=1 \quad\text{and}\quad \frac{x^2}{a}+\frac{y^2}{b}=a+b$$

represent ellipses with the same foci and that, if their eccentricities are e_1, e_2, respectively, then $e_1 = e_2\surd(2-e_2^2)$.

39. Prove that, if p_1, p_2 are the perpendicular distances of the foci S, S' of the ellipse $x^2/a^2+y^2/b^2 = 1$ from any tangent to the ellipse, then $p_1p_2 = b^2$. [Use $x = a\cos\theta$, $y = b\sin\theta$.]

40. [Reflection property of an ellipse.] If P is any point on an ellipse with foci S, S', prove that PS, PS' are equally inclined to the normal at P to the ellipse.

41. A fixed circle has centre C, and A is a fixed point within the circle. If QR is a chord through A, the point in which CR meets the line through A parallel to CQ is denoted by P. Show that all such points P lie on a fixed ellipse.

42. If a curve has equation $5x^2-6xy+5y^2 = 8$ with respect to rectangular axes Ox, Oy, find its equation with respect to rectangular axes $O\xi$, $O\eta$, where $\angle xO\xi = \frac{1}{4}\pi$. Deduce that the curve is an ellipse, and find the coordinates of its foci relative to the axes Ox, Oy.

43. Show that the equation $4x^2-y^2-24x-4y+12 = 0$ represents a hyperbola and find the coordinates of its foci and the equations of its asymptotes.

44. In the usual notation for a hyperbola, A is the point (5, 0) and X the point (3, 0), and the latus rectum of the hyperbola has length 15. Show that the hyperbola has eccentricity 3/2 and find the coordinates of its centre C. Find the equation of the hyperbola and the equations of its asymptotes.

45. Show that, if c is a positive real number, the hyperbola with eccentricity $\surd 2$ which has a focus $S(c\surd 2,\ c\surd 2)$ and corresponding directrix $x+y = c\surd 2$ has equation $xy = c^2$. Sketch the hyperbola, showing the axes of symmetry and the asymptotes.

46. A hyperbola H has centre C and a focus S, and the line through S perpendicular to the transverse axis meets the asymptotes in F and F'. An ellipse E has foci F and F' and passes through C. If the eccentricities of H and E are e_1 and e_2, respectively, show that $e_2^2 = (e_1^2-1)/e_1^2$.

47. If a curve has equation $x^2-4xy-2y^2 = 6$ with respect to rectangular axes Ox, Oy, find its equation with respect to rectangular axes $O\xi$, $O\eta$, where $\angle xO\xi = \cos^{-1}(1/\surd 5)$. Deduce that the curve is a hyperbola, and find the equations of its axes. What is the relation between this curve and that of problem **23**?

48. Show that the rectangular hyperbola $xy = c^2$ (see Example **45**) has parametric equations $x = ct$, $y = c/t$, $t \neq 0$. Show that:

(i) the chord joining points $P_1(t_1)$ and $P_2(t_2)$ has equation
$x+t_1t_2y = c(t_1+t_2)$,

(ii) the tangent at point $P(t)$ has equation $x+t^2y = 2ct$,

(iii) if the tangent at $P(t)$ meets the asymptotes at M and N, then P is the midpoint of MN,

(iv) the tangents at the points $P(t)$, $Q(3/t)$ meet on the line $x = 3y$,

(v) if the vertices of a triangle lie on the hyperbola, so does the orthocentre of the triangle.

Part 2

Three-dimensional Geometry

Three-dimensional Geometry

2

1. Coordinates in 3-dimensional euclidean space

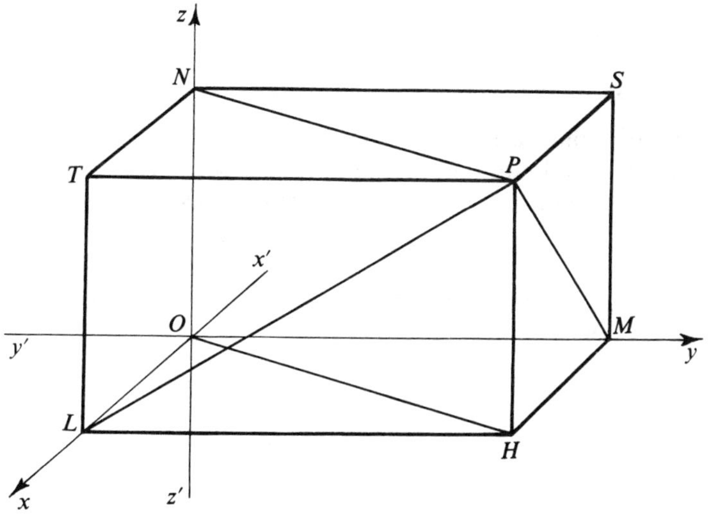

In setting up a coordinate system, we take three mutually perpendicular directed lines $x'x$, $y'y$, $z'z$ intersecting at a point O and forming a right-handed system. [If a person stands at O facing the direction $\overrightarrow{Oy}$ with his head towards $\overrightarrow{Oz}$, then direction $\overrightarrow{Ox}$ is to his *right*.] We choose a unit of length. If P is any point in space $\neq O$, we form the brick or cuboid with O and P as opposite vertices and with three edges along the lines $x'x$, $y'y$, $z'z$. If L, M, N are the vertices which are the projections of P on the directed lines $x'x$, $y'y$, $z'z$, respectively, and if $x = OL$, $y = OM$, $z = ON$, then x, y, z are called the x-, y- and z-coordinates of P in the **coordinate system** consisting of x-**axis** $x'x$, y-**axis** $y'y$, z-**axis** $z'z$, **origin** O and given unit of length. We say that P is the point with coordinates (x, y, z); we often use the notation (x_P, y_P, z_P) for these coordinates. The origin O has coordinates $(0, 0, 0)$.

The eight vertices of the **coordinate brick** shown in the figure, with their coordinates, are as follows:

$P(x, y, z)$ and the origin $O(0, 0, 0)$;

$L(x, 0, 0)$, $M(0, y, 0)$, $N(0, 0, z)$, the projections of P on $x'x$, $y'y$, $z'z$;

$H(x, y, 0)$, $S(0, y, z)$, $T(x, 0, z)$, the projections of P on the planes xOy, yOz and zOx, respectively.

The planes xOy, yOz and zOx are respectively called the x, y-**plane,** the y, z-**plane** and the z, x-**plane.**

The coordinate planes divide space into eight regions, called the eight **octants,** which can be listed as follows:

$$\begin{aligned}
\text{the first octant, } Oxyz, &= \{(x, y, z): x>0, y>0, z>0\},\\
\text{the second octant, } Ox'yz, &= \{(x, y, z): x<0, y>0, z>0\},\\
\text{the third octant, } Ox'y'z, &= \{(x, y, z): x<0, y<0, z>0\},\\
\text{the fourth octant, } Oxy'z, &= \{(x, y, z): x>0, y<0, z>0\},
\end{aligned}$$

and similarly four octants with $z<0$.

There is a bijection from space to the set $\{(x, y, z): x, y, z\in \mathbf{R}\}$, i.e. $\mathbf{R}^3$, by mapping the point P to its triple of coordinates (x, y, z).

The distance formula.

Theorem 2.1. *If A has coordinates (x_A, y_A, z_A) and B has coordinates (x_B, y_B, z_B), then*

$$|AB| = \sqrt{\{(x_B-x_A)^2+(y_B-y_A)^2+(z_B-z_A)^2\}}.$$

Proof.

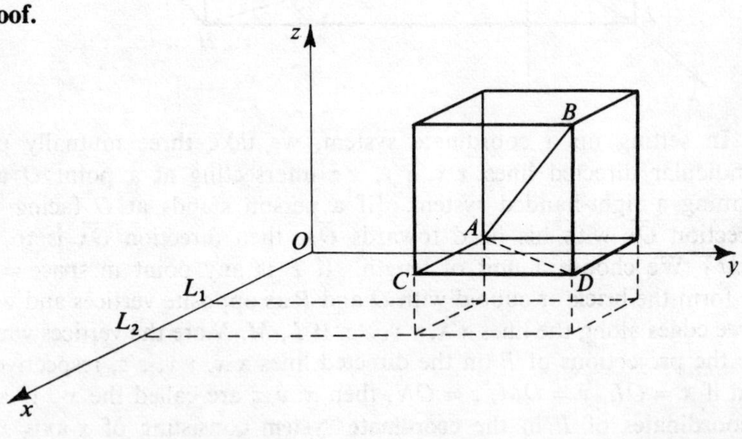

The diagram shows the brick with A, B as opposite vertices and faces parallel to the coordinate planes. In the figure, by using the theorem of Pythagoras,

$$|AB|^2 = |AD|^2+|DB|^2 = |AC|^2+|CD|^2+|DB|^2.$$

Now $|AC|^2 = (L_1L_2)^2 = (x_B-x_A)^2$, where L_1, L_2 are the projections of A and B on $x'x$. Similarly, by projecting on $y'y$ and on $z'z$, we can show that $|CD|^2 = (y_B-y_A)^2$ and $|DB|^2 = (z_B-z_A)^2$.

Thus $$|AB|^2 = (x_B-x_A)^2+(y_B-y_A)^2+(z_B-z_A)^2,$$

and from this the required result follows.

Corollary. If P is the point (x, y, z) and O is the origin, then

$$|OP| = \sqrt{(x^2+y^2+z^2)}.$$

Example 1. Show that the triangle with vertices $A(2, 1, 3)$, $B(3, 0, 5)$, $C(5, -4, 2)$ is right-angled.

$|AB|^2 = 1+1+4 = 6$; $|AC|^2 = 9+25+1 = 35$; $|BC|^2 = 4+16+9 = 29$.

Thus $|AB|^2+|BC|^2 = |AC|^2$, and so, by the converse of the theorem of Pythagoras, the triangle is right-angled at B.

The section formulae. *If P is a point on the line determined by points A and B ($P \neq B$) and if $AP:PB = m:n$, then*

$$x_P = \frac{mx_B+nx_A}{m+n},\quad y_P = \frac{my_B+ny_A}{m+n},\quad z_P = \frac{mz_B+nz_A}{m+n}. \tag{1.1}$$

Proof. If L_1, L_2, L_3 are the projections of the points A, P, B on the x-axis, then

$$\frac{m}{n} = \frac{AP}{PB} = \frac{L_1L_2}{L_2L_3} = \frac{x_P-x_A}{x_B-x_P}.$$

Thus

$$mx_B-mx_P = nx_P-nx_A,$$

so that

$$x_P = \frac{mx_B+nx_A}{m+n}.$$

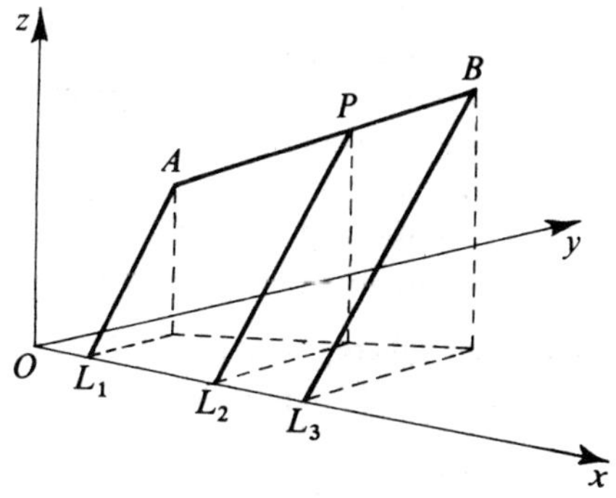

Similarly, by projecting on the y-axis and the z-axis, we obtain the expressions for y_P and z_P.

Corollary. The midpoint of $\overrightarrow{AB}$ has coordinates

$$\left(\tfrac{1}{2}(x_A+x_B),\ \tfrac{1}{2}(y_A+y_B),\ \tfrac{1}{2}(z_A+z_B)\right).$$

This result follows from (1.1) by taking $m = n = 1$.

Example 2. Find the coordinates of the centroid G of triangle ABC.
If A' is the midpoint of side BC, then

$$\frac{AG}{GA'} = \frac{2}{1}.$$

Now A' is the point $\left(\tfrac{1}{2}(x_B+x_C),\ \tfrac{1}{2}(y_B+y_C),\ \tfrac{1}{2}(z_B+z_C)\right)$; thus

$$x_G = \frac{2x_{A'}+x_A}{2+1} = \frac{1}{3}(x_A+x_B+x_C).$$

Similarly, $y_G = \tfrac{1}{3}(y_A+y_B+y_C)$ and $z_G = \tfrac{1}{3}(z_A+z_B+z_C)$.

2. Some simple loci in space (with a given coordinate system)

I. The coordinate planes and parallel planes. The x, y-plane is the set of points $\{(x, y, z): z = 0\}$; a point (x, y, z) lies in the plane if and only if $z = 0$. The plane has equation $z = 0$.

Any plane parallel to the x, y-plane has equation of the form $z = k$ for some real number k.

Similarly, the y, z-plane has equation $x = 0$ and any parallel plane has equation of the form $x = k$ for some real k. Also the z, x-plane has equation $y = 0$ and any parallel plane has equation of the form $y = k$ for some real k.

II. The coordinate axes. The x-axis is the set of points $\{(x, y, z): y = 0, z = 0\}$, so that the x-axis is determined by the pair of equations $y = z = 0$. A point lies on the x-axis if and only if its coordinates are of the form $(k, 0, 0)$ for some real k.

Similarly, the y-axis is given by the pair of equations $x = z = 0$ and a point lies on the y-axis if and only if it has coordinates of the form $(0, k, 0)$ for some real k. Also the z-axis is given by the equations $x = y = 0$ and a point lies on the z-axis if and only if it has coordinates of the form $(0, 0, k)$ for some real k.

III. The sphere, centre $C(a, b, c)$ and radius r.
This is the set of points

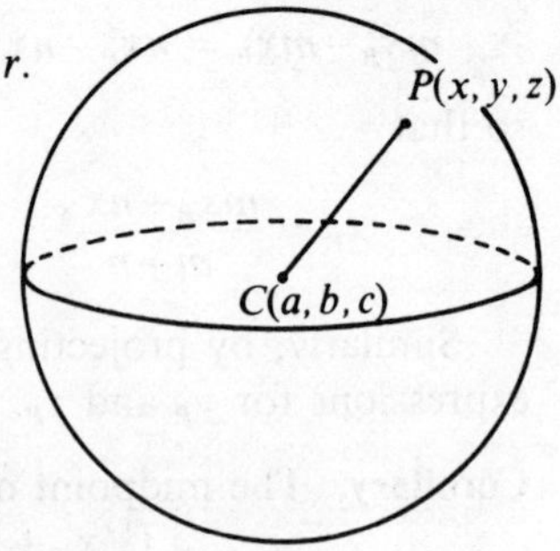

$$\begin{aligned} &\{P: |CP| = r\} \\ &= \{P: |CP|^2 = r^2\} \\ &= \{(x, y, z): (x-a)^2+(y-b)^2+(z-c)^2 = r^2\}. \end{aligned}$$

Thus the sphere has equation

$$(x-a)^2+(y-b)^2+(z-c)^2 = r^2. \qquad (2.1)$$

This equation is of the form

$$x^2+y^2+z^2+2ux+2vy+2wz+d = 0.$$

IV. *If* $u^2+v^2+w^2-d \geqslant 0$, *the equation*

$$x^2+y^2+z^2+2ux+2vy+2wz+d=0 \tag{2.2}$$

represents a sphere.

Proof. The set $\{(x, y, z): x^2+y^2+z^2+2ux+2vy+2wz+d=0\}$ $= \{(x,y,z): (x-(-u))^2+(y-(-v))^2+(z-(-w))^2 = u^2+v^2+w^2-d\}$, and so, by (2.1), equation (2.2) represents the sphere with centre $(-u, -v, -w)$ and radius $\sqrt{(u^2+v^2+w^2-d)}$.

When $u^2+v^2+w^2-d=0$, equation (2.2) represents the set $\{(-u, -v, -w)\}$, i.e. the single point $(-u, -v, -w)$; this is often called a **point sphere.** When $u^2+v^2+w^2-d<0$, equation (2.2) represents the empty set.

V. The **interior of the sphere** with centre $C(a, b, c)$ and radius r is

$$\{P: |CP|<r\} = \{(x, y, z): (x-a)^2+(y-b)^2+(z-c)^2<r^2\}$$
$$= \{(x, y, z): (x-a)^2+(y-b)^2+(z-c)^2-r^2<0\},$$

and the **exterior of this sphere** is

$$\{P: |CP|>r\} = \{(x, y, z): (x-a)^2+(y-b)^2+(z-c)^2-r^2>0\}.$$

VI. The cylinder with generators parallel to the z-axis which cuts the x, y-plane in the curve with equation $f(x,y)=0$ in that plane.

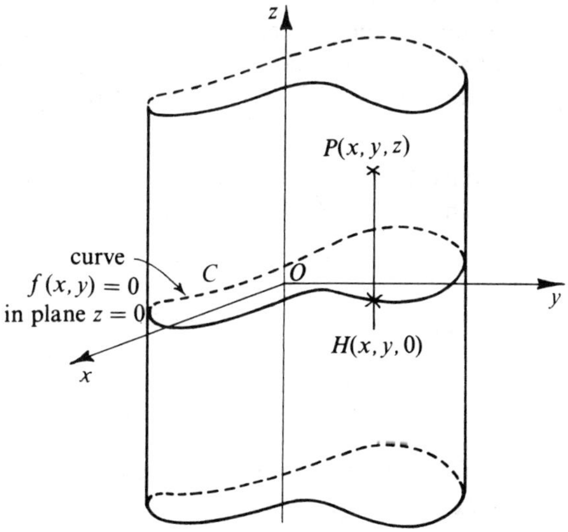

A **cylinder** is a surface formed by drawing through each point of a fixed curve the line parallel to a fixed given line. The set of parallel lines is the set of **generators** of the cylinder.

For the surface given, a point $P(x, y, z)$ lies on the cylinder if and only if its projection $H(x, y, 0)$ on the x, y-plane lies on the curve C, and so, if and only if $f(x, y)=0$. Hence the cylinder has equation $f(x, y)=0$.

Similar results hold for cylinders with generators parallel to the x-axis or parallel to the y-axis.

A cylinder that often appears is the right circular cylinder with the z-axis as axis of symmetry and circular cross-section of radius r. This cylinder has equation $x^2+y^2 = r^2$.

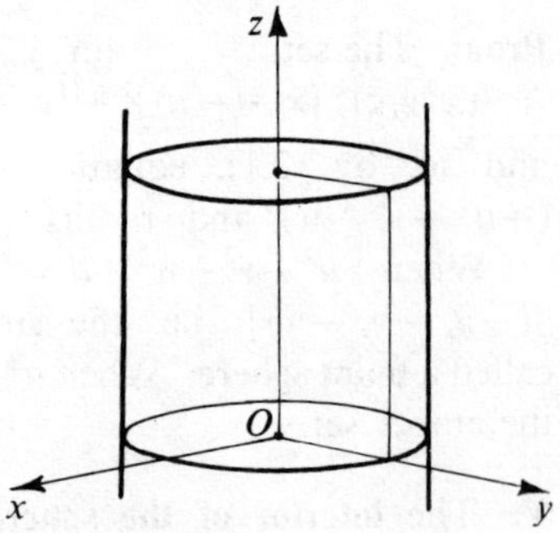

In particular, the right circular cylinder with the z-axis as axis of symmetry and cross-section of radius 1 has equation $x^2+y^2 = 1$.

Exercise. Sketch the cylinders with equations (i) $x^2+y^2-2x=0$, (ii) $x^2+y^2-2by=0$, b a positive constant, (iii) $y^2+z^2 = 1$, (iv) $z^2+x^2 = 1$.

Example 1. Find the equation of the sphere on AB as diameter, where A is the point $(-1, 0, 2)$ and B is the point $(3, 4, -6)$. Find the length of the intercept cut by the sphere on the z-axis.

The centre of the sphere is the point $C(1, 2, -2)$, the midpoint of $\overrightarrow{AB}$, and the radius of the sphere is $|CA| = \sqrt{(4+4+16)} = \sqrt{(24)}$. Hence the sphere has equation $(x-1)^2+(y-2)^2+(z+2)^2 = 24$.

The sphere meets the z-axis where $x = y = 0$. Thus the points of intersection of the sphere with the z-axis are given by the equation $1+4+(z+2)^2 = 24$, and so by $z = -2\pm\sqrt{(19)}$. Consequently the points are $E(0, 0, -2-\sqrt{(19)})$ and $F(0, 0, -2+\sqrt{(19)})$. The intercept cut on the z-axis has length $EF = 2\sqrt{(19)}$.

Example 2. If A is the point $(-1, 0, -2)$ and B the point $(2, -3, 1)$, identify the set $\{P : |AP| = 2|BP|\}$.

The set is the subset of points

$$\{(x, y, z) : (x+1)^2+y^2+(z+2)^2 = 4[(x-2)^2+(y+3)^2+(z-1)^2]\}$$
$$= \{(x, y, z) : x^2+y^2+z^2+2x+4z+5 = 4[x^2+y^2+z^2-4x+6y-2z+14]\}$$
$$= \{(x, y, z) : 3(x^2+y^2+z^2)-18x+24y-12z+51 = 0\}$$
$$= \{(x, y, z) : x^2+y^2+z^2-6x+8y-4z+17 = 0\}$$
$$= \{(x, y, z) : (x-3)^2+(y+4)^2+(z-2)^2 = 12\}.$$

Thus the set of points is the sphere with centre $C(3, -4, 2)$ and radius $2\sqrt{3}$.

Example 3. Find the equations of the two spheres which touch the z-axis and pass through the circle

$$x^2+y^2-4x-6y+1 = 0, \quad z = 0, \tag{2.3}$$

i.e. the circle in which the plane $z = 0$ cuts the right-circular cylinder $x^2+y^2-4x-6y+1 = 0$.

The sphere

$$x^2+y^2+z^2+2ux+2vy+2wz+d = 0 \tag{2.4}$$

meets the plane $z = 0$ where

$$x^2+y^2+2ux+2vy+d = 0.$$

Hence the sphere (2.4) passes through circle (2.3) if and only if $u = -2$, $v = -3$ and $d = 1$, and so, if and only if its equation is of the form

$$x^2+y^2+z^2-4x-6y+2wz+1 = 0. \tag{2.5}$$

The sphere with equation (2.5) meets the z-axis at points where $x = y = 0$, and so where $z^2+2wz+1 = 0$; it touches the z-axis if and only if equation $z^2+2wz+1 = 0$ has equal roots, i.e. $\Leftrightarrow w = \pm 1$. It follows that the two spheres satisfying the given conditions have equations

$$x^2+y^2+z^2-4x-6y+2z+1 = 0$$

and

$$x^2+y^2+z^2-4x-6y-2z+1 = 0.$$

3. Vectors

In order to deal with direction in space we introduce the idea of a vector. In physics, the word *vector* is used for physical terms such as velocity, acceleration, or force. Each of these has (1) a magnitude in terms of a unit of measure and (2) a direction in space. In geometry, a line-segment $\overrightarrow{AB}$, with initial point A and end point B, has associated with it (1) its length $|AB|$ in terms of a given unit of length and (2) the direction $A \to B$. Consequently we use for the definition of a vector a definition that covers all of these situations.

Definition. A **non-zero vector** is a combination of two things:

(1) a positive real number, called the **magnitude** or **length** of the vector,

(2) a direction in space.

We can express such a vector as an ordered pair $(a, \mathscr{D})$, where a is a positive real number and $\mathscr{D}$ a direction in space.

The exceptional **zero vector** has magnitude 0, but no direction.

Vectors will be denoted by symbols such as $\boldsymbol{a}$, $\boldsymbol{b}$, $\boldsymbol{u}$, $\boldsymbol{v}$, . . . , and the zero vector by $\boldsymbol{0}$. The magnitude of $\boldsymbol{u}$ is denoted by $|\boldsymbol{u}|$.

Equality of vectors. Two vectors $\boldsymbol{u}$, $\boldsymbol{v}$ are said to be **equal vectors** if they have the same magnitude and the same direction; we write $\boldsymbol{u} = \boldsymbol{v}$ when $\boldsymbol{u}$, $\boldsymbol{v}$ are equal. [This definition of equality is that used in vector geometry. In physics other definitions may have to be used; e.g. $\boldsymbol{u} = \boldsymbol{v}$ if $\boldsymbol{u}$, $\boldsymbol{v}$ have the same magnitude and the same direction along the same line.]

Geometrical representations of vectors. Let $\boldsymbol{u}$ be a given non-zero vector. If A, B are points in space such that

(1) $|AB| = |\boldsymbol{u}|$,

(2) the direction of $\overrightarrow{AB}$ is the direction of $\boldsymbol{u}$,

then the line-segment $\overrightarrow{AB}$ is called a **geometrical representation** of $\boldsymbol{u}$. When $\overrightarrow{AB}$ is a geometrical representation of $\boldsymbol{u}$, for convenience we call $\overrightarrow{AB}$ itself a vector and write $\overrightarrow{AB} = \boldsymbol{u}$.

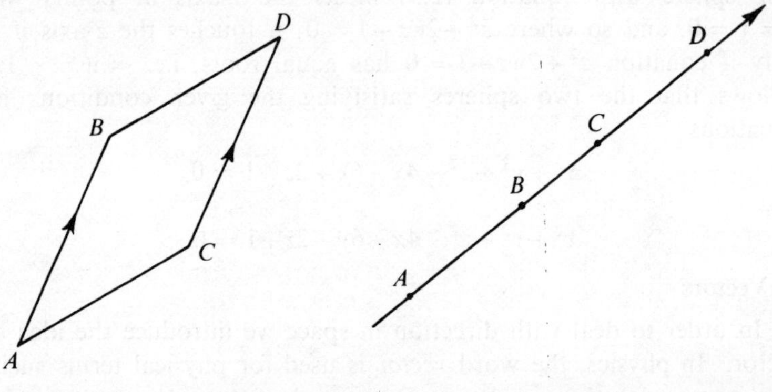

If $\overrightarrow{CD}$ is another geometrical representation of the vector $\boldsymbol{u}$, then $\overrightarrow{AB}$ and $\overrightarrow{CD}$ have the same length and the same direction. Thus, as indicated in the diagram, either $ABDC$ is a parallelogram or A, B, C, D are collinear and $AB = CD$ relative to the common direction of $\overrightarrow{AB}$ and $\overrightarrow{CD}$; we write $\overrightarrow{AB} = \overrightarrow{CD} = \boldsymbol{u}$.

If A is a point in space, $\overrightarrow{AA}$ may be taken to represent the zero vector $\boldsymbol{0}$.

If $\boldsymbol{u}$ is a given vector and A a given point in space, then there is a unique vector $\overrightarrow{AB}$ with initial point A such that $\overrightarrow{AB} = \boldsymbol{u}$.

Addition of vectors. Let $\boldsymbol{u}$, $\boldsymbol{v}$ be any two vectors and let $\overrightarrow{AB}$ and $\overrightarrow{BC}$ be representations of $\boldsymbol{u}$ and $\boldsymbol{v}$, respectively, so that the end point of the line-segment representing $\boldsymbol{u}$ is the initial point of that representing $\boldsymbol{v}$. Then the vector $\boldsymbol{u}+\boldsymbol{v}$ is defined to be that represented by $\overrightarrow{AC}$, i.e. $\boldsymbol{u}+\boldsymbol{v} = \overrightarrow{AC}$.

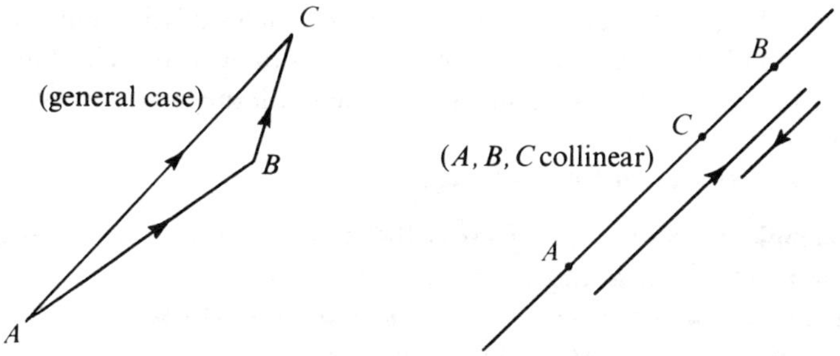

We write $\overrightarrow{AB}+\overrightarrow{BC} = \overrightarrow{AC}$.

This definition of addition of vectors is, by congruence and parallelism, independent of the initial point A chosen.

The collinear case is the one-dimensional case considered in Section **1** of Part **1**.

If $\boldsymbol{v} = \boldsymbol{0}$, then $\boldsymbol{u}+\boldsymbol{0} = \overrightarrow{AB}+\overrightarrow{BB} = \overrightarrow{AB} = \boldsymbol{u}$, and $\boldsymbol{0}+\boldsymbol{u} = \overrightarrow{AA}+\overrightarrow{AB} = \overrightarrow{AB} = \boldsymbol{u}$.

Also $\overrightarrow{AB}+\overrightarrow{BA} = \overrightarrow{AA} = \boldsymbol{0}$, so that $\boldsymbol{u}+\overrightarrow{BA} = \boldsymbol{0}$. For this reason we denote the vector represented by $\overrightarrow{BA}$ by $-\boldsymbol{u}$ and call this the **negative** of $\boldsymbol{u}$. Thus $\boldsymbol{u}+(-\boldsymbol{u}) = \boldsymbol{0}$. We also have:

$$(-\boldsymbol{u})+(\boldsymbol{u}) = \overrightarrow{BA}+\overrightarrow{AB} = \overrightarrow{BB} = \boldsymbol{0}; \quad -(-\boldsymbol{u}) = -\overrightarrow{BA} = \overrightarrow{AB} = \boldsymbol{u}.$$

Properties of addition of vectors. For all vectors $\boldsymbol{u}$, $\boldsymbol{v}$, $\boldsymbol{w}$ we have:

(i) $\boldsymbol{u}+\boldsymbol{v} = \boldsymbol{v}+\boldsymbol{u}$ (commutative property);
(ii) $\boldsymbol{u}+(\boldsymbol{v}+\boldsymbol{w}) = (\boldsymbol{u}+\boldsymbol{v})+\boldsymbol{w}$ (associative property);
(iii) $\boldsymbol{u}+\boldsymbol{0} = \boldsymbol{u} = \boldsymbol{0}+\boldsymbol{u}$;
(iv) $\boldsymbol{u}+(-\boldsymbol{u}) = \boldsymbol{0} = (-\boldsymbol{u})+\boldsymbol{u}$.

Proofs of (i) and (ii)

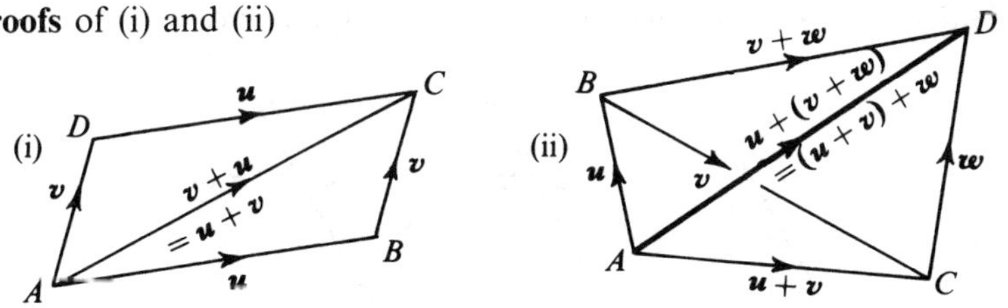

Proofs for the non-collinear case are obtained at once from an examination of the geometrical representations indicated in the diagrams. The collinear cases are also easily checked from geometrical representations.

Notes 1. We usually write $\boldsymbol{u}+\boldsymbol{v}+\boldsymbol{w}$ for both sides of (ii). This notation can be extended to a sum of any finite number of vectors. The expression $\boldsymbol{u}_1+\boldsymbol{u}_2+\ldots+\boldsymbol{u}_n$ has a value independent of the order in which the additions are performed.

2. We write $\boldsymbol{v}-\boldsymbol{u}$ for $\boldsymbol{v}+(-\boldsymbol{u})$.

Example 1. Show that $\boldsymbol{v}-\boldsymbol{u}$ is the unique solution of the equation $\boldsymbol{x}+\boldsymbol{u}=\boldsymbol{v}$, in which $\boldsymbol{u}$ and $\boldsymbol{v}$ are given vectors.

Since $(\boldsymbol{v}-\boldsymbol{u})+\boldsymbol{u}=(\boldsymbol{v}+(-\boldsymbol{u}))+\boldsymbol{u}=\boldsymbol{v}+((-\boldsymbol{u})+\boldsymbol{u})=\boldsymbol{v}+\boldsymbol{0}=\boldsymbol{v}$, it follows that $\boldsymbol{v}-\boldsymbol{u}$ is a solution of the equation.

Also, if $\boldsymbol{x}$ is any solution, then

$$\boldsymbol{x}+\boldsymbol{u}=\boldsymbol{v}\Rightarrow(\boldsymbol{x}+\boldsymbol{u})+(-\boldsymbol{u})=\boldsymbol{v}+(-\boldsymbol{u})\Rightarrow\boldsymbol{x}+(\boldsymbol{u}+(-\boldsymbol{u}))=\boldsymbol{v}-\boldsymbol{u}$$
$$\Rightarrow\boldsymbol{x}+\boldsymbol{0}=\boldsymbol{v}-\boldsymbol{u}\Rightarrow\boldsymbol{x}=\boldsymbol{v}-\boldsymbol{u},$$

and the result follows.

The triangle inequality. The magnitude of a vector satisfies the inequality

$$|\boldsymbol{u}+\boldsymbol{v}|\leqslant|\boldsymbol{u}|+|\boldsymbol{v}|,$$

(called the **triangle inequality** for vectors); for, if $\overrightarrow{AB}=\boldsymbol{u}$ and $\overrightarrow{BC}=\boldsymbol{v}$, then $\overrightarrow{AC}=\boldsymbol{u}+\boldsymbol{v}$, and consequently

$$|\boldsymbol{u}+\boldsymbol{v}|=|\overrightarrow{AC}|\leqslant|\overrightarrow{AB}|+|\overrightarrow{BC}|=|\boldsymbol{u}|+|\boldsymbol{v}|.$$

Equality holds if and only if A, B, C are collinear and B lies on the line-segment $\overrightarrow{AC}$.

Multiplication of a vector by a scalar, i.e. **by a real number.** [In physics the word *scalar* is used for physical terms like kinetic energy which have a magnitude only; in geometry a scalar is a real number.]

Definition. Let $\boldsymbol{u}$ be a non-zero vector and p a non-zero scalar.

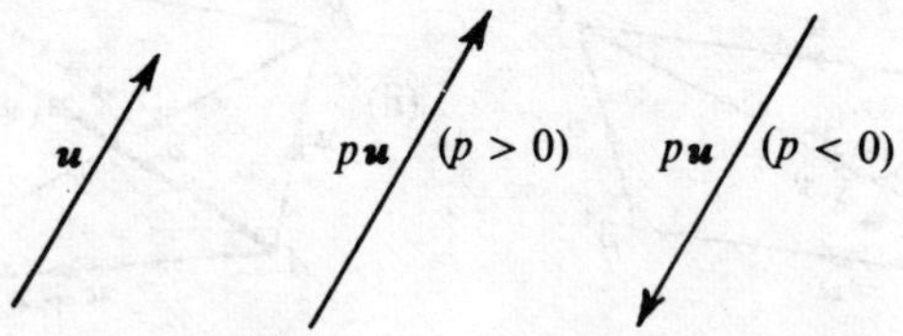

The vector whose magnitude is $|p||\boldsymbol{u}|$ and whose direction is that of $\boldsymbol{u}$ if p is positive, and that of $-\boldsymbol{u}$ if p is negative, is denoted by $p\boldsymbol{u}$ and called the **scalar multiple** of $\boldsymbol{u}$ by p.

We define $p\boldsymbol{0}$ and $0\boldsymbol{u}$, for any p and $\boldsymbol{u}$ respectively, to be $\boldsymbol{0}$.

Some properties of scalar multiples. Using geometrical representations, the following properties can be proved [(vi) holds by definition]:

(i) $(p+q)\boldsymbol{u} = p\boldsymbol{u}+q\boldsymbol{u}$ (iv) $1\boldsymbol{u} = \boldsymbol{u}$

(ii) $p(\boldsymbol{u}+\boldsymbol{v}) = p\boldsymbol{u}+p\boldsymbol{v}$ (v) $(-1)\boldsymbol{u} = -\boldsymbol{u}$

(iii) $p(q\boldsymbol{u}) = (pq)\boldsymbol{u}$ (vi) $p\boldsymbol{0} = \boldsymbol{0} = 0\boldsymbol{u}$

The reader should investigate these proofs.

Unit vectors. A vector $\boldsymbol{u}$ of magnitude 1 is called a **unit vector**, i.e. a vector for which $|\boldsymbol{u}| = 1$.

Any non-zero vector $\boldsymbol{u}$ can be expressed in two ways as a scalar multiple of a unit vector; for,

$$\boldsymbol{u} = |\boldsymbol{u}|\frac{\boldsymbol{u}}{|\boldsymbol{u}|} = (-|\boldsymbol{u}|)\left(-\frac{\boldsymbol{u}}{|\boldsymbol{u}|}\right) \quad \text{and} \quad \frac{\boldsymbol{u}}{|\boldsymbol{u}|},\ -\frac{\boldsymbol{u}}{|\boldsymbol{u}|}$$

are unit vectors, since

$$\left|\frac{\boldsymbol{u}}{|\boldsymbol{u}|}\right| = \left|-\frac{\boldsymbol{u}}{|\boldsymbol{u}|}\right| = \frac{|\boldsymbol{u}|}{|\boldsymbol{u}|} = 1.$$

Note. If $\overrightarrow{AB} = \boldsymbol{u}$ and $\overrightarrow{AC} = \boldsymbol{v}$, then $\boldsymbol{v}$ is a scalar multiple of $\boldsymbol{u}$, say $\boldsymbol{v} = p\boldsymbol{u}$, if and only if A, B, C are collinear and $\overrightarrow{AC} = p\overrightarrow{AB}$.

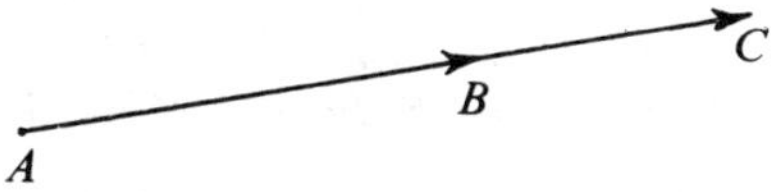

4. Geometrical applications of addition and scalar multiples of vectors

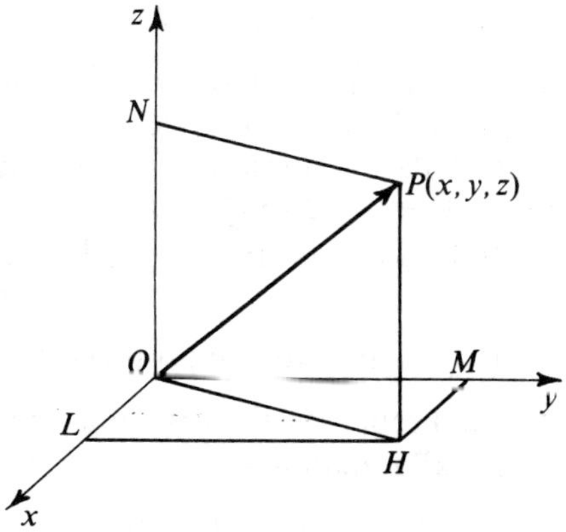

We take a rectangular co-ordinate system determined by axes Ox, Oy, Oz. If $P(x, y, z)$ is a point in space, the vector $\overrightarrow{OP}$ is called the **position vector** of P with respect to the origin O; it is often denoted by $\boldsymbol{r}_P$ or simply $\boldsymbol{r}$. We find a very useful expression for $\boldsymbol{r}_P$ in terms of x, y, z and the unit vectors $\boldsymbol{i}$, $\boldsymbol{j}$, $\boldsymbol{k}$ in the directions $\overrightarrow{Ox}$, $\overrightarrow{Oy}$, $\overrightarrow{Oz}$, respectively, as follows: If L, M, N, H are the projections of P on the x-axis, y-axis, z-axis and x, y-plane, respectively, then

$$\begin{aligned} \boldsymbol{r}_P = \overrightarrow{OP} = \overrightarrow{OH}+\overrightarrow{HP} &= \overrightarrow{OL}+\overrightarrow{LH}+\overrightarrow{HP} \\ &= \overrightarrow{OL}+\overrightarrow{OM}+\overrightarrow{ON} \\ &= x\boldsymbol{i}+y\boldsymbol{j}+z\boldsymbol{k}, \end{aligned}$$

noting that $OL = x$, $OM = y$ and $ON = z$.

We call x, y, z the **components** of $\overrightarrow{OP}$ with respect to the vectors $\boldsymbol{i}, \boldsymbol{j}, \boldsymbol{k}$; we often write $\overrightarrow{OP} = (x, y, z)$ as a shorthand notation for $\overrightarrow{OP} = x\boldsymbol{i}+y\boldsymbol{j}+z\boldsymbol{k}$; note that $|\overrightarrow{OP}| = \sqrt{(x^2+y^2+z^2)}$.

If $\boldsymbol{u}$ is any vector, then there is a unique vector $\overrightarrow{OP} = \boldsymbol{u}$, and hence there are *unique* real numbers x, y, z such that $\boldsymbol{u} = x\boldsymbol{i}+y\boldsymbol{j}+z\boldsymbol{k}$. The numbers x, y, z are called the **components** of $\boldsymbol{u}$ with respect to the vectors $\boldsymbol{i}, \boldsymbol{j}, \boldsymbol{k}$, and we often write $\boldsymbol{u} = (x, y, z)$; note that $|\boldsymbol{u}| = |\overrightarrow{OP}| = \sqrt{(x^2+y^2+z^2)}$.

The following theorem expresses in component form the basic ideas of equality, addition, subtraction and multiplication by a scalar for vectors. The vectors $\boldsymbol{i}, \boldsymbol{j}, \boldsymbol{k}$ in this work and in later work will always mean the unit vectors in the directions $\overrightarrow{Ox}, \overrightarrow{Oy}, \overrightarrow{Oz}$ of a given coordinate system.

Theorem 2.2. *If* $\boldsymbol{u} = x_1\boldsymbol{i}+y_1\boldsymbol{j}+z_1\boldsymbol{k}$ and $\boldsymbol{v} = x_2\boldsymbol{i}+y_2\boldsymbol{j}+z_2\boldsymbol{k}$, *then*

(i) $\boldsymbol{u} = \boldsymbol{v} \Leftrightarrow x_1 = x_2,\ y_1 = y_2$ and $z_1 = z_2$,

(ii) $\boldsymbol{u}+\boldsymbol{v} = (x_1+x_2)\boldsymbol{i}+(y_1+y_2)\boldsymbol{j}+(z_1+z_2)\boldsymbol{k}$,

(iii) $\boldsymbol{u}-\boldsymbol{v} = (x_1-x_2)\boldsymbol{i}+(y_1-y_2)\boldsymbol{j}+(z_1-z_2)\boldsymbol{k}$,

(iv) $p\boldsymbol{u} = px_1\boldsymbol{i}+py_1\boldsymbol{j}+pz_1\boldsymbol{k}$, *for any scalar* p.

Proof. (i) Part (i) follows from the uniqueness of components.

(ii)
$$\begin{aligned} \boldsymbol{u}+\boldsymbol{v} &= x_1\boldsymbol{i}+y_1\boldsymbol{j}+z_1\boldsymbol{k}+x_2\boldsymbol{i}+y_2\boldsymbol{j}+z_2\boldsymbol{k} \\ &= (x_1\boldsymbol{i}+x_2\boldsymbol{i})+(y_1\boldsymbol{j}+y_2\boldsymbol{j})+(z_1\boldsymbol{k}+z_2\boldsymbol{k}) \\ &= (x_1+x_2)\boldsymbol{i}+(y_1+y_2)\boldsymbol{j}+(z_1+z_2)\boldsymbol{k}, \end{aligned}$$

using properties of addition and scalar multiples of vectors at each stage. [Indicate the property used at each step.]

(iii) Part (iii) follows from (ii) by noting that $\boldsymbol{u}-\boldsymbol{v} = \boldsymbol{u}+(-\boldsymbol{v})$ and that $-\boldsymbol{v} = -x_2\boldsymbol{i}-y_2\boldsymbol{j}-z_2\boldsymbol{k}$.

(iv)
$$\begin{aligned} p\boldsymbol{u} = p(x_1\boldsymbol{i}+y_1\boldsymbol{j}+z_1\boldsymbol{k}) &= p(x_1\boldsymbol{i})+p(y_1\boldsymbol{j})+p(z_1\boldsymbol{k}) \\ &= px_1\boldsymbol{i}+py_1\boldsymbol{j}+pz_1\boldsymbol{k}. \end{aligned}$$

[Again indicate the property used at each step.]

Note. Properties (i), (ii), (iii), (iv) have the following equivalents in "triples" notation:

(i) $(x_1, y_1, z_1) = (x_2, y_2, z_2) \Leftrightarrow x_1 = x_2,\ y_1 = y_2$ and $z_1 = z_2$,

(ii) $(x_1, y_1, z_1)+(x_2, y_2, z_2) = (x_1+x_2,\ y_1+y_2,\ z_1+z_2)$,

(iii) $(x_1, y_1, z_1) - (x_2, y_2, z_2) = (x_1 - x_2,\ y_1 - y_2,\ z_1 - z_2)$,
(iv) $p(x_1, y_1, z_1) = (px_1, py_1, pz_1)$.

The simple result contained in the next theorem is one of the key results for the use of vectors in geometry.

Theorem 2.3. *If $\boldsymbol{r}_A$, $\boldsymbol{r}_B$ are the position vectors of the points A, B with respect to an origin O, then*

$$\vec{AB} = \boldsymbol{r}_B - \boldsymbol{r}_A.$$

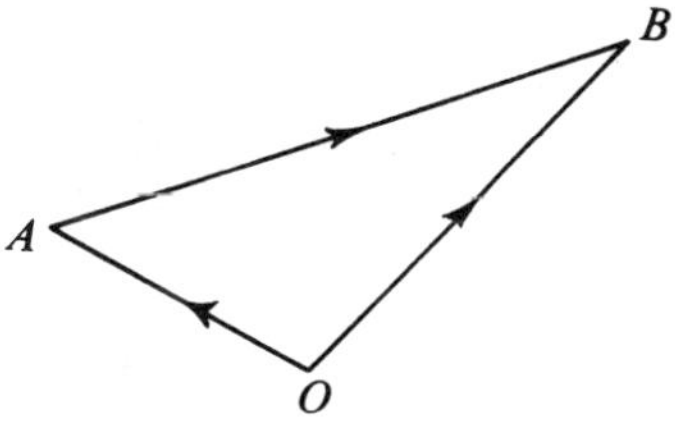

Proof.

$$\vec{OA} + \vec{AB} = \vec{OB}.$$

Thus

$$\vec{AB} = \vec{OB} - \vec{OA} = \boldsymbol{r}_B - \boldsymbol{r}_A.$$

Note. From Theorem 2.3 we obtain at once the following statement involving components.

If $\boldsymbol{r}_A = x_1\boldsymbol{i} + y_1\boldsymbol{j} + z_1\boldsymbol{k}$ and $\boldsymbol{r}_B = x_2\boldsymbol{i} + y_2\boldsymbol{j} + z_2\boldsymbol{k}$, then

$$\vec{AB} = (x_2 - x_1)\boldsymbol{i} + (y_2 - y_1)\boldsymbol{j} + (z_2 - z_1)\boldsymbol{k},$$

so that $\vec{AB}$ has components $x_2 - x_1$, $y_2 - y_1$, $z_2 - z_1$ with respect to $\boldsymbol{i}, \boldsymbol{j}, \boldsymbol{k}$.

In "triples" notation: If $\boldsymbol{r}_A = (x_1, y_1, z_1)$ and $\boldsymbol{r}_B = (x_2, y_2, z_2)$, then $\vec{AB} = (x_2 - x_1,\ y_2 - y_1,\ z_2 - z_1)$. This can also be expressed in the following form: If A is the point (x_1, y_1, z_1) and B the point (x_2, y_2, z_2), then $\vec{AB} = (x_2 - x_1)\boldsymbol{i} + (y_2 - y_1)\boldsymbol{j} + (z_2 - z_1)\boldsymbol{k}$ or, in "triples" notation, $\vec{AB} = (x_2 - x_1, y_2 - y_1, z_2 - z_1)$.

By the distance formula of Section **1**,

$$|\vec{AB}| = \sqrt{\{(x_2 - x_1)^2 + (y_2 - y_1)^2 + (z_2 - z_1)^2\}}.$$

The section formula. *If P is the point on the line determined by the points A and B such that $AP:PB = m:n$, then*

$$\boldsymbol{r}_P = \frac{1}{m+n}(m\boldsymbol{r}_B + n\boldsymbol{r}_A). \tag{4.1}$$

Proof. From the definition of scalar multiple and position ratio,

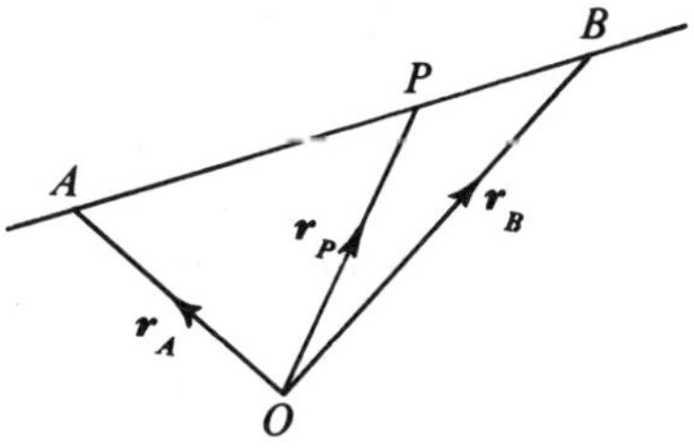

$$\vec{AP} = \frac{m}{n}\vec{PB};$$

consequently,

$$n(\boldsymbol{r}_P - \boldsymbol{r}_A) = m(\boldsymbol{r}_B - \boldsymbol{r}_P),$$

so that $(m+n)\boldsymbol{r}_P = m\boldsymbol{r}_B + n\boldsymbol{r}_A$, from which the required result (4.1) easily follows.

Midpoint of $\overrightarrow{AB}$. Taking $m = n = 1$ in (4.1), we deduce that the mid-point of $\overrightarrow{AB}$ has position vector $\frac{1}{2}(\boldsymbol{r}_A + \boldsymbol{r}_B)$.

Exercise. Write (4.1) in component form and compare with the two-dimensional result in Section **2** of Part **1**.

Example 1. If L, M, N are the midpoints of the sides BC, CA, AB of a triangle ABC and O is any point, show that (i) $\overrightarrow{OA}+\overrightarrow{OB}+\overrightarrow{OC} = \overrightarrow{OL}+\overrightarrow{OM}+\overrightarrow{ON}$, (ii) $\overrightarrow{AL}+\overrightarrow{BM}+\overrightarrow{CN} = \boldsymbol{0}$.

Now $\boldsymbol{r}_L = \frac{1}{2}(\boldsymbol{r}_B+\boldsymbol{r}_C)$, $\boldsymbol{r}_M = \frac{1}{2}(\boldsymbol{r}_C+\boldsymbol{r}_A)$, $\boldsymbol{r}_N = \frac{1}{2}(\boldsymbol{r}_A+\boldsymbol{r}_B)$; thus

$$\overrightarrow{OL}+\overrightarrow{OM}+\overrightarrow{ON} = \boldsymbol{r}_L+\boldsymbol{r}_M+\boldsymbol{r}_N = \boldsymbol{r}_A+\boldsymbol{r}_B+\boldsymbol{r}_C = \overrightarrow{OA}+\overrightarrow{OB}+\overrightarrow{OC}.$$

Also,
$$\begin{aligned}\overrightarrow{AL}+\overrightarrow{BM}+\overrightarrow{CN} &= (\boldsymbol{r}_L-\boldsymbol{r}_A)+(\boldsymbol{r}_M-\boldsymbol{r}_B)+(\boldsymbol{r}_N-\boldsymbol{r}_C)\\ &= (\boldsymbol{r}_L+\boldsymbol{r}_M+\boldsymbol{r}_N)-(\boldsymbol{r}_A+\boldsymbol{r}_B+\boldsymbol{r}_C) = \boldsymbol{0}.\end{aligned}$$

Direction cosines and direction numbers for a line. Each direction in space is uniquely determined by the unit vector in that direction, and in particular, by the unit vector $\overrightarrow{OU}$ in that direction through a given origin O. The vector $\overrightarrow{OU}$ is completely specified by the angles $\angle xOU$, $\angle yOU$, $\angle zOU$ which $\overrightarrow{OU}$ makes with the directions $\overrightarrow{Ox}$, $\overrightarrow{Oy}$, $\overrightarrow{Oz}$, and so with the unit vectors $\boldsymbol{i}, \boldsymbol{j}, \boldsymbol{k}$. These angles will be called the **direction angles** for the given direction with respect to the given coordinate system; their radian measures will be denoted by α, β, γ and we shall use the intervals $0 \leqslant \alpha \leqslant \pi$, $0 \leqslant \beta \leqslant \pi$, $0 \leqslant \gamma \leqslant \pi$.

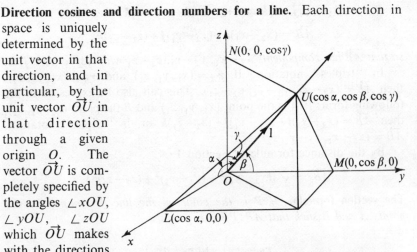

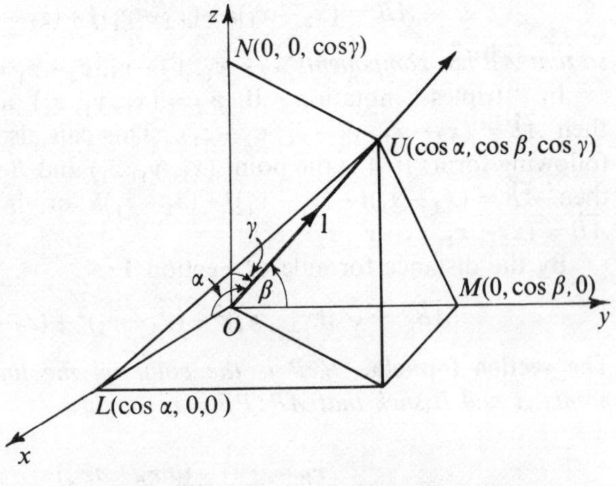

If L, M, N are the projections of U on the x, y and z-axes, respectively, then, by the definition of the cosine function,

$$\frac{OL}{OU} = \cos\alpha, \quad \frac{OM}{OU} = \cos\beta, \quad \frac{ON}{OU} = \cos\gamma,$$

and so $\qquad OL = \cos\alpha,\ OM = \cos\beta,\ ON = \cos\gamma.$

Hence $\qquad \vec{OL} = \cos\alpha\boldsymbol{i},\ \vec{OM} = \cos\beta\boldsymbol{j},\ \vec{ON} = \cos\gamma\boldsymbol{k}$

and $\qquad \vec{OU} = \cos\alpha\boldsymbol{i}+\cos\beta\boldsymbol{j}+\cos\gamma\boldsymbol{k}.$

The components $\cos\alpha$, $\cos\beta$, $\cos\gamma$ of the unit vector $\vec{OU}$ are called the **direction cosines** of the direction determined by $\vec{OU}$ (or simply of $\vec{OU}$) with respect to the given coordinate system. The point U has coordinates $(\cos\alpha, \cos\beta, \cos\gamma)$.

Since $|\vec{OU}| = 1$, we have:

$$\cos^2\alpha+\cos^2\beta+\cos^2\gamma = 1.$$

The unit vector $-\vec{OU} = \vec{UO}$ has direction cosines $\cos(\pi-\alpha)$, $\cos(\pi-\beta)$, $\cos(\pi-\gamma)$, i.e. $-\cos\alpha$, $-\cos\beta$, $-\cos\gamma$.

Note. $\boldsymbol{i}$, $\boldsymbol{j}$, $\boldsymbol{k}$ have direction cosines $(1, 0, 0)$, $(0, 1, 0)$ and $(0, 0, 1)$, respectively.

Example 2. If a direction makes an angle $\frac{1}{3}\pi$ with $\boldsymbol{i}$ and $\boldsymbol{j}$, what angle does it make with the unit vector $\boldsymbol{k}$?

If this angle is γ, then $\cos^2\frac{1}{3}\pi+\cos^2\frac{1}{3}\pi+\cos^2\gamma = 1$; thus

$$\cos^2\gamma = 1-2(\tfrac{1}{2})^2 = \tfrac{1}{2}, \text{ so that } \cos\gamma = \pm 1/\sqrt{2}.$$

It follows that there are two such directions, one with $\gamma = \frac{1}{4}\pi$ and the other with $\gamma = \frac{3}{4}\pi$. [Indicate the directions in a diagram.]

Direction numbers for the direction of $\vec{OU} = \cos\alpha\boldsymbol{i}+\cos\beta\boldsymbol{j}+\cos\gamma\boldsymbol{k}$. Any triple of real numbers l, m, n, not all zero, are called **direction numbers** for the direction of $\vec{OU}$ if there exists a number k such that $l = k\cos\alpha$, $m = k\cos\beta$, $n = k\cos\gamma$, i.e. such that

$$\frac{l}{\cos\alpha} = \frac{m}{\cos\beta} = \frac{n}{\cos\gamma} = k.$$

Then $\qquad l^2+m^2+n^2 = k^2(\cos^2\alpha+\cos^2\beta+\cos^2\gamma) = k^2, \qquad$ so that $k = \pm\sqrt{(l^2+m^2+n^2)}$.

It follows that a triple of real numbers l, m, n, not all zero, determines two sets of direction cosines (and so two unit vectors), namely

$$\left(\frac{l, m, n}{\sqrt{(l^2+m^2+n^2)}}\right) \text{ and } \left(\frac{-l, -m, -n}{\sqrt{(l^2+m^2+n^2)}}\right),$$

using an obvious compact notation. In particular, if the point $A(\neq O)$ has coordinates (a, b, c), then the direction cosines of $\vec{OA}$ and $\vec{AO}$ are, respectively,

$$\left(\frac{a, b, c}{\sqrt{(a^2+b^2+c^2)}}\right) \text{ and } \left(\frac{-a, -b, -c}{\sqrt{(a^2+b^2+c^2)}}\right).$$

Direction numbers and cosines for the line determined by the points A, B.

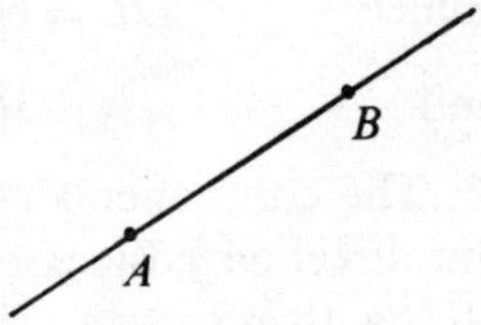

The components $(x_B - x_A,\ y_B - y_A,\ z_B - z_A)$ of $\vec{AB} = (x_B - x_A)\boldsymbol{i} + (y_B - y_A)\boldsymbol{j} + (z_B - z_A)\boldsymbol{k}$ are direction numbers for the direction of $\vec{AB}$ and the corresponding direction cosines are

$$\left(\frac{x_B - x_A,\ y_B - y_A,\ z_B - z_A}{\sqrt{\{(x_B - x_A)^2 + (y_B - y_A)^2 + (z_B - z_A)^2\}}}\right),$$

i.e. the components of the unit vector $\vec{AB}/|\vec{AB}|$.

Similarly, the direction of $\vec{BA}$ has direction numbers $x_A - x_B$, $y_A - y_B$, $z_A - z_B$ and has as direction cosines the components of the unit vector $\vec{BA}/|\vec{BA}|$.

Note. In dealing with lines it is often convenient to use the phrase "*direction numbers l, m, n* (*or cosines*) *for a given line L*". This means that l, m, n are direction numbers (or cosines) for one of the two directions of L. Then kl, km, kn, for any real number $k \neq 0$, are also direction numbers for L. To determine such numbers we need only take two points A, B on L and obtain the components of $\vec{AB}$ or $\vec{BA}$.

Example 3. Find direction cosines for the line determined by the points $A(1, -1, 0)$ and $B(3, 2, -1)$.

$\vec{AB} = (2, 3, -1)$ and $|\vec{AB}| = \sqrt{(4+9+1)} = \sqrt{(14)}$. Thus the line has direction cosines

$$\left(\frac{2}{\sqrt{(14)}}, \frac{3}{\sqrt{(14)}}, \frac{-1}{\sqrt{(14)}}\right).$$

[$\vec{BA} = (-2, -3, 1)$, so that the other possible set of direction cosines is

$$\left(\frac{-2}{\sqrt{(14)}}, \frac{-3}{\sqrt{(14)}}, \frac{1}{\sqrt{(14)}}\right);$$

the line has direction numbers $(2t, 3t, -t)$ for any $t \neq 0$.]

Vector equation of line through the point A determined by the direction of unit vector $\boldsymbol{u}$.

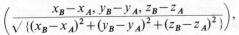

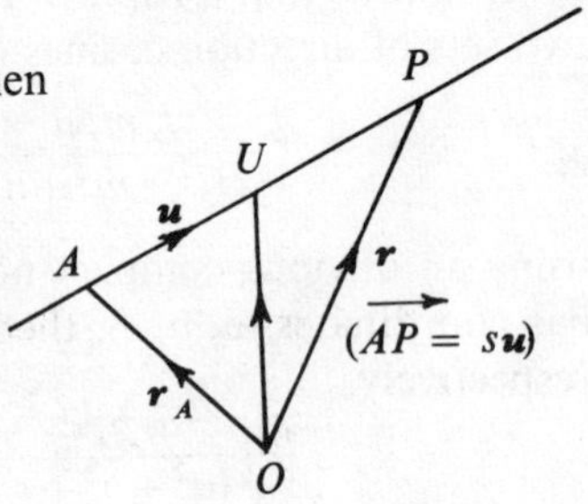

If $\vec{OA} = \boldsymbol{r}_A$, $\vec{AU} = \boldsymbol{u}$ and $\vec{OP} = \boldsymbol{r}$, then

$$P \in \text{the line} \Leftrightarrow \vec{AP} = AP\boldsymbol{u},$$

where AP is the measure of $\vec{AP}$ relative to the direction of $\boldsymbol{u}$. Thus

$$P \in \text{the line} \Leftrightarrow \boldsymbol{r} - \boldsymbol{r}_A = s\boldsymbol{u}, \text{ where } s = AP,$$

$$\Leftrightarrow \boldsymbol{r} = \boldsymbol{r}_A + s\boldsymbol{u}.$$

The line is the set of points $\{\boldsymbol{r}:\boldsymbol{r} = \boldsymbol{r}_A + s\boldsymbol{u},\ s\in\mathbf{R}\}$; s is a **parameter** (or variable) for the line in the sense that each value of s gives a point on the line, and each point on the line gives rise to a unique value of s, called the parameter of that point. For example, $s = 0$ gives the point A and $s = 1$ gives the point U.

The equation

$$\boldsymbol{r} = \boldsymbol{r}_A + s\boldsymbol{u} \tag{4.2}$$

is called the vector equation for the line.

Note. If $\boldsymbol{u}$ is *not* a *unit* vector, then in this case we have:

$$\begin{aligned} P\in\text{the line} &\Leftrightarrow \overrightarrow{AP} = t\boldsymbol{u} \quad \text{for some } t\in\mathbf{R}, \\ &\Leftrightarrow \boldsymbol{r}-\boldsymbol{r}_A = t\boldsymbol{u}, \\ &\Leftrightarrow \boldsymbol{r} = \boldsymbol{r}_A + t\boldsymbol{u}. \end{aligned} \tag{4.3}$$

The line is the set of points $\{\boldsymbol{r}:\boldsymbol{r} = \boldsymbol{r}_A + t\boldsymbol{u},\ t\in\mathbf{R}\}$, but in this case, the parameter t does *not* denote signed distance along the line; the line has vector equation (4.3).

If $\boldsymbol{r} = x\boldsymbol{i}+y\boldsymbol{j}+z\boldsymbol{k}$, $\boldsymbol{r}_A = x_1\boldsymbol{i}+y_1\boldsymbol{j}+z_1\boldsymbol{k}$ and $\boldsymbol{u} = l\boldsymbol{i}+m\boldsymbol{j}+n\boldsymbol{k}$, so that l, m, n are direction numbers (or cosines) for the line, then, from (4.3),

$$(x, y, z) = (x_1+tl,\ y_1+tm,\ z_1+tn),$$

and so

$$x = x_1+tl,\ y = y_1+tm,\ z = z_1+tn. \tag{4.4}$$

This set of equations can be written in the form

$$\frac{x-x_1}{l} = \frac{y-y_1}{m} = \frac{z-z_1}{n} = t. \tag{4.5}$$

Equations (4.4) are called **parametric equations** for the line, and (4.5) equations for the line in **symmetric form.** The parameter t denotes signed distance along the line with respect to the direction of (l, m, n) if and only if (l, m, n) is a *unit* vector.

The line determined by the points $A(\boldsymbol{a})$, $B(\boldsymbol{b})$. Here the line passes through the point A and is determined by the direction of $\overrightarrow{AB}$.

$$\overrightarrow{AB} = \boldsymbol{b}-\boldsymbol{a}.$$

$$\begin{aligned} P(\boldsymbol{r})\in\text{the line} &\Leftrightarrow \overrightarrow{AP} = t\overrightarrow{AB} \text{ for some } t\in\mathbf{R}, \\ &\Leftrightarrow \boldsymbol{r}-\boldsymbol{a} = t(\boldsymbol{b}-\boldsymbol{a}), \\ &\Leftrightarrow \boldsymbol{r} = (1-t)\boldsymbol{a}+t\boldsymbol{b}. \end{aligned} \tag{4.6}$$

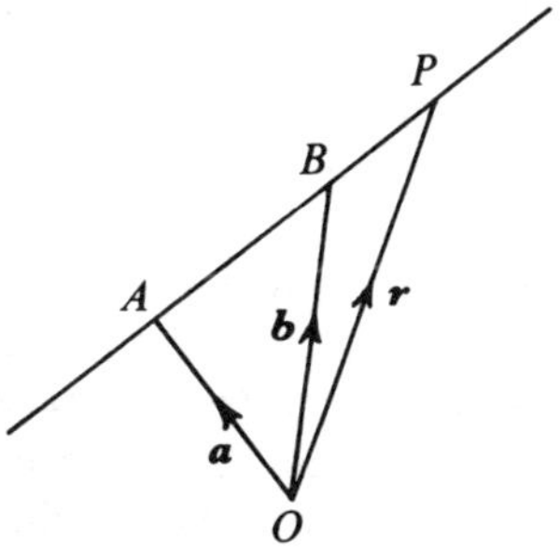

Thus, with t a parameter on $\mathbf{R}$, (4.6) is the vector equation of the line.

[$t = 0$ gives A and $t = 1$ gives B; what is the parameter of the midpoint of $\overrightarrow{AB}$?]

Example 4. Find equations corresponding to (4.3) (or (4.6)), (4.4) and (4.5) for the line determined by the points $A(1, 9, 5)$ and $B(3, 5, 7)$. Find the points at which the line AB meets the coordinate planes.

$$\overrightarrow{AB} = (2, -4, 2) = 2(1, -2, 1),$$

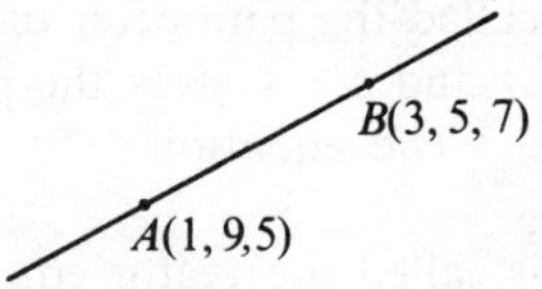

so that 1, −2, 1 are direction numbers for the line. The line has vector equation

$$\boldsymbol{r} = (x, y, z) = \boldsymbol{r}_A + t(1, -2, 1), \quad (t \in \mathbf{R})$$

i.e. $$\boldsymbol{r} = (x, y, z) = (1, 9, 5) + (t, -2t, t) = (1+t, 9-2t, 5+t).$$

Consequently the line has parametric equations

$$x = 1+t, \quad y = 9-2t, \quad z = 5+t \quad (t \in \mathbf{R}),$$

[A is given by $t = 0$, B is given by $t = 2$.]

and symmetric equations

$$\frac{x-1}{1} = \frac{y-9}{-2} = \frac{z-5}{1} = t.$$

The line meets the x, y-plane where $z = 0$ and so at the point with parameter t given by $5+t = 0$, i.e. $t = -5$; this point has coordinates $(-4, 19, 0)$. Similarly it meets the plane $x = 0$ where $t = -1$ and so at the point $(0, 11, 4)$ and meets the plane $y = 0$ where $t = 9/2$ and so at the point $(11/2, 0, 19/2)$.

Example 5. Determine which of the following sets of points are collinear

(i) $A(1, 2, 3)$, $B(0, 3, 2)$, $C(3, 0, 5)$;

(ii) $P(1, 3, 4)$, $Q(5, 5, 6)$, $R(9, 9, 8)$.

(i) $\overrightarrow{AB} = (-1, 1, -1)$, $\overrightarrow{AC} = (2, -2, 2) = -2\overrightarrow{AB}$, and so A, B, C are collinear; also $CA : AB = 2 : 1$.

(ii) $\overrightarrow{PQ} = (4, 2, 2)$, $\overrightarrow{PR} = (8, 6, 4) = 2(4, 3, 2) \neq t\overrightarrow{PQ}$ for any $t \in \mathbf{R}$. Hence P, Q, R are *not* collinear.

Coplanar vectors. If $\boldsymbol{u}$, $\boldsymbol{v}$ are *non-zero* and *non-parallel* vectors and if $\overrightarrow{OA} = \boldsymbol{u}$ and $\overrightarrow{OB} = \boldsymbol{v}$, then the plane AOB or any parallel plane is called a plane determined by the vectors $\boldsymbol{u}$, $\boldsymbol{v}$. A vector $\boldsymbol{w}$ is said to be **coplanar** with $\boldsymbol{u}$ and $\boldsymbol{v}$ if $\boldsymbol{w}$ can be represented by a line-segment in the planes determined by $\boldsymbol{u}$ and $\boldsymbol{v}$. The word **non-coplanar** will be used to describe three (or more) vectors which are not coplanar. If three vectors are non-coplanar, then each pair of the vectors determines a plane in which the third vector does not lie.

Theorem 2.4 *A vector* $\boldsymbol{w}$ *is coplanar with the non-zero, non-parallel vectors* $\boldsymbol{u}$, $\boldsymbol{v}$ *if and only if there exist scalars* a, b *such that*

$$\boldsymbol{w} = a\boldsymbol{u}+b\boldsymbol{v}, \tag{4.7}$$

[i.e. such that $\boldsymbol{w}$ is a sum of multiples of $\boldsymbol{u}$ and $\boldsymbol{v}$].

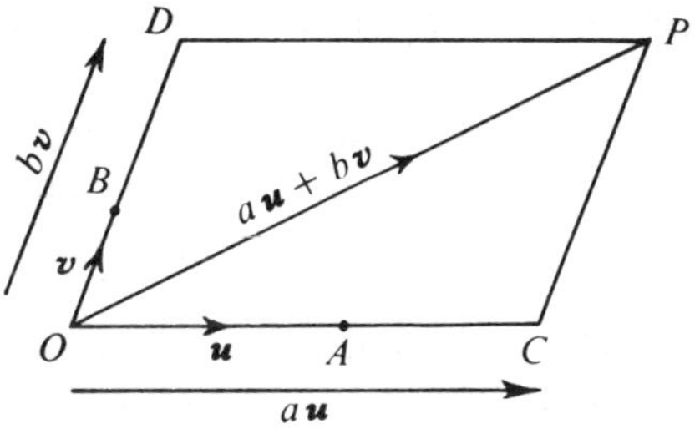

Proof. Suppose in the first place that $\boldsymbol{w} = a\boldsymbol{u}+b\boldsymbol{v}$ for some scalars a, b.

If $\overrightarrow{OA} = \boldsymbol{u}$, $\overrightarrow{OB} = \boldsymbol{v}$, $a\boldsymbol{u} = \overrightarrow{OC}$ and $b\boldsymbol{v} = \overrightarrow{OD}$, and if the line through C parallel to $\boldsymbol{v}$ meets the line through D parallel to $\boldsymbol{u}$, at P, then $\overrightarrow{OP} = \overrightarrow{OC}+\overrightarrow{CP} = a\boldsymbol{u}+b\boldsymbol{v} = \boldsymbol{w}$; thus $\boldsymbol{w}$ is coplanar with $\boldsymbol{u}$ and $\boldsymbol{v}$.

Conversely, suppose now that $\boldsymbol{w}$ is coplanar with $\boldsymbol{u}$ and $\boldsymbol{v}$, and let $\overrightarrow{OA} = \boldsymbol{u}$, $\overrightarrow{OB} = \boldsymbol{v}$ and $\overrightarrow{OP} = \boldsymbol{w}$. If C and D are the points on the lines OA and OB such that $OCPD$ is a parallelogram, then $\overrightarrow{OC} = a\boldsymbol{u}$ and $\overrightarrow{OD} = b\boldsymbol{v}$ for some scalars a, b. Hence $\boldsymbol{w} = \overrightarrow{OP} = \overrightarrow{OC}+\overrightarrow{CP} = a\boldsymbol{u}+b\boldsymbol{v}$, and the result follows.

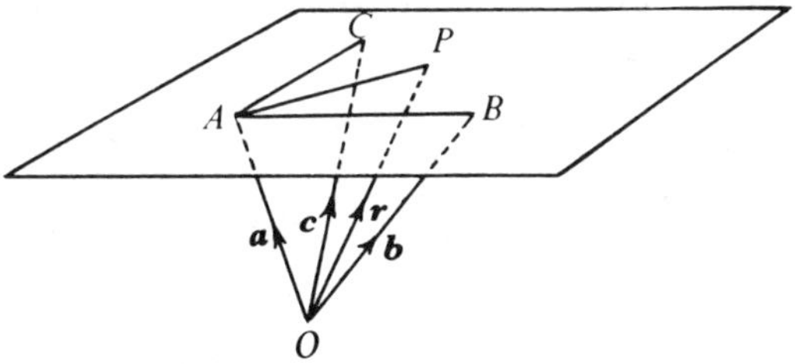

Vector equation of the plane determined by the points A, B, C **with position vectors** $\boldsymbol{a}$, $\boldsymbol{b}$, $\boldsymbol{c}$.

The plane is determined by the non-zero, non-parallel vectors $\overrightarrow{AB}$ and $\overrightarrow{AC}$.

$P(\boldsymbol{r}) \in$ the planc

$$\begin{aligned}
&\Leftrightarrow \overrightarrow{AP} \text{ is coplanar with } \overrightarrow{AB} \text{ and } \overrightarrow{AC}\\
&\Leftrightarrow \overrightarrow{AP} = s\overrightarrow{AB}+t\overrightarrow{AC} \text{ for some real numbers } s,\ t\\
&\Leftrightarrow \boldsymbol{r}-\boldsymbol{a} = s(\boldsymbol{b}-\boldsymbol{a})+t(\boldsymbol{c}-\boldsymbol{a})\\
&\Leftrightarrow \boldsymbol{r} = (1-s-t)\boldsymbol{a}+s\boldsymbol{b}+t\boldsymbol{c}.
\end{aligned} \tag{4.8}$$

This equation, with the two parameters s and t, is the vector equation of the plane.

[The point A is given by $s = t = 0$; B is given by $s = 1$, $t = 0$ and C by $s = 0$, $t = 1$. The centroid of triangle ABC is given by $s = t = \frac{1}{3}$.]

Example 6. Show that the six planes each passing through one edge of a tetrahedron and the midpoint of the opposite edge meet in a point.

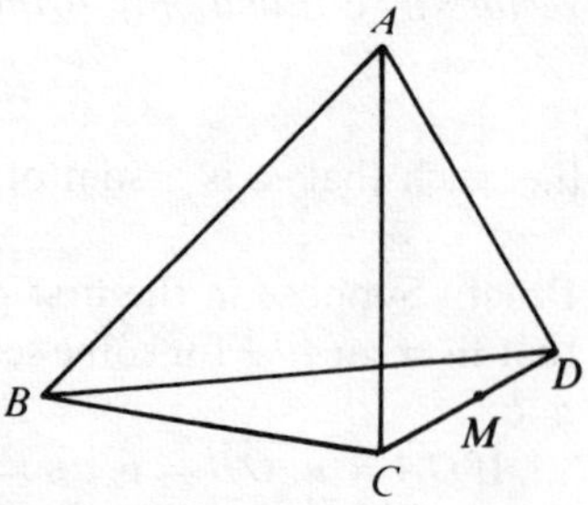

If the vertices A, B, C, D have position vectors $\boldsymbol{a}$, $\boldsymbol{b}$, $\boldsymbol{c}$, $\boldsymbol{d}$ with respect to an origin O, then the midpoint M of edge CD has position vector $\frac{1}{2}(\boldsymbol{c}+\boldsymbol{d})$.

From (4.8), the plane through the edge AB and the point M has equation

$$\boldsymbol{r} = (1-s-t)\boldsymbol{a}+s\boldsymbol{b}+\tfrac{1}{2}t(\boldsymbol{c}+\boldsymbol{d}), \text{ with } s,\ t \text{ as parameters.}$$

The result will follow if we show that this plane passes through a point whose position vector is symmetrical in $\boldsymbol{a}$, $\boldsymbol{b}$, $\boldsymbol{c}$, $\boldsymbol{d}$. We require $1-s-t = s = \frac{1}{2}t$, and so $t = 2s$ and $1-3s = s$, giving $s = \frac{1}{4}$ and $t = \frac{1}{2}$. These parametric values show that the point $\frac{1}{4}(\boldsymbol{a}+\boldsymbol{b}+\boldsymbol{c}+\boldsymbol{d})$ lies on the plane. Since by symmetry this point lies also on the five other similar planes, the result follows.

Vector bases. We begin by proving the following result.

Theorem 2.5. *If $\boldsymbol{u}$, $\boldsymbol{v}$, $\boldsymbol{w}$ are non-coplanar vectors, then every vector $\boldsymbol{a}$ can be expressed uniquely in the form $a_1\boldsymbol{u}+a_2\boldsymbol{v}+a_3\boldsymbol{w}$ with a_1, a_2, a_3 real numbers.*

Proof. Take $\overrightarrow{OA} = \boldsymbol{u}$, $\overrightarrow{OB} = \boldsymbol{v}$, $\overrightarrow{OC} = \boldsymbol{w}$ and $\overrightarrow{OP} = \boldsymbol{a}$, and complete the *parallelepiped* indicated in the diagram with faces parallel to the planes determined by the vectors $\boldsymbol{u}$, $\boldsymbol{v}$, $\boldsymbol{w}$ in pairs. Then

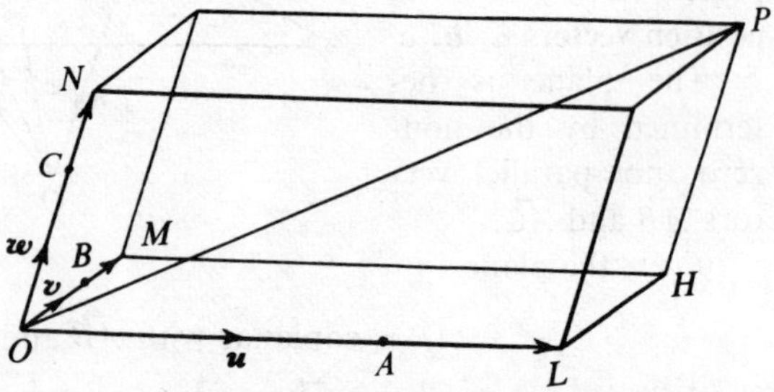

$$\boldsymbol{a} = \overrightarrow{OP} = \overrightarrow{OL}+\overrightarrow{LH}+\overrightarrow{HP} = \overrightarrow{OL}+\overrightarrow{OM}+\overrightarrow{ON} = a_1\boldsymbol{u}+a_2\boldsymbol{v}+a_3\boldsymbol{w},$$

where a_1, a_2, a_3 are the real numbers given by $\overrightarrow{OL} = a_1\overrightarrow{OA}$, $\overrightarrow{OM} = a_2\overrightarrow{OB}$ and $\overrightarrow{ON} = a_3\overrightarrow{OC}$.

We now show that this expression for $\boldsymbol{a}$ is unique. Suppose that we also have $\boldsymbol{a} = b_1\boldsymbol{u}+b_2\boldsymbol{v}+b_3\boldsymbol{w}$ with $b_3 \neq a_3$, say.

Then $a_1\boldsymbol{u}+a_2\boldsymbol{v}+a_3\boldsymbol{w} = b_1\boldsymbol{u}+b_2\boldsymbol{v}+b_3\boldsymbol{w}$,

so that $(b_3-a_3)\boldsymbol{w} = (a_1-b_1)\boldsymbol{u}+(a_2-b_2)\boldsymbol{v}$.

Consequently,
$$\boldsymbol{w} = \frac{a_1-b_1}{b_3-a_3}\boldsymbol{u}+\frac{a_2-b_2}{b_3-a_3}\boldsymbol{v}.$$

This implies, by Theorem 2.4, that $\boldsymbol{u}$, $\boldsymbol{v}$, $\boldsymbol{w}$ are coplanar. Since this is contrary to the fact that $\boldsymbol{u}$, $\boldsymbol{v}$, $\boldsymbol{w}$ are non-coplanar, it follows that $a_3 = b_3$. Similarly $a_1 = b_1$ and $a_2 = b_2$, and the result follows.

Definition. A set of three non-zero vectors $\boldsymbol{u}$, $\boldsymbol{v}$, $\boldsymbol{w}$, which has the property that every vector $\boldsymbol{a}$ can be expressed uniquely in the form $\boldsymbol{a} = a_1\boldsymbol{u}+a_2\boldsymbol{v}+a_3\boldsymbol{w}$ with a_1, a_2, a_3 real numbers, is said to form a **basis** for 3-dimensional euclidean space.

Theorem 2.5 shows that every triple of non-coplanar vectors forms a basis for space. A simple example of such a set is the set $\{\boldsymbol{i}, \boldsymbol{j}, \boldsymbol{k}\}$ of the usual coordinate unit vectors.

Components with respect to a basis. If $\{\boldsymbol{u}, \boldsymbol{v}, \boldsymbol{w}\}$ is a basis for space and if $\boldsymbol{a} = a_1\boldsymbol{u}+a_2\boldsymbol{v}+a_3\boldsymbol{w}$, then the coefficients a_1, a_2, a_3 are called the **components** of the vector $\boldsymbol{a}$ with respect to the (ordered) basis $\boldsymbol{u}$, $\boldsymbol{v}$, $\boldsymbol{w}$. The basis provides a coordinate system for space, the axes being in general oblique. If $\boldsymbol{a} = \overrightarrow{OP}$, then P has coordinates (a_1, a_2, a_3) in the coordinate system with origin O provided by the vectors $\boldsymbol{u}$, $\boldsymbol{v}$, $\boldsymbol{w}$.

Algebraic test for a basis. An important test for a basis that is easy to apply is provided by the following result.

Theorem 2.6. *The non-zero vectors* $\boldsymbol{u}$, $\boldsymbol{v}$, $\boldsymbol{w}$ *are non-coplanar if and only if they satisfy the following condition*:

$$x\boldsymbol{u}+y\boldsymbol{v}+z\boldsymbol{w} = \boldsymbol{0} \Rightarrow x = 0, y = 0, z = 0 \quad (x, y, z \text{ scalars}). \qquad (4.9)$$

Vectors $\boldsymbol{u}$, $\boldsymbol{v}$, $\boldsymbol{w}$ satisfying the condition (4.9) are said to be **linearly independent.** Vectors $\boldsymbol{u}$, $\boldsymbol{v}$, $\boldsymbol{w}$ for which (4.9) does *not* hold are called **linearly dependent**; in this case there is a linear relation $x\boldsymbol{u}+y\boldsymbol{v}+z\boldsymbol{w} = \boldsymbol{0}$ with scalars x, y, z not all zero.

Note. From Theorems **2.5** and **2.6** it follows that, if vectors $\boldsymbol{u}$, $\boldsymbol{v}$, $\boldsymbol{w}$ are linearly independent, then they form a basis for space. It is left as an exercise to check, from the definitions of a basis and linear independence, that the converse is also true. [See the first part of the following proof.]

Proof of Theorem 2.6. (i) Suppose that $\boldsymbol{u}$, $\boldsymbol{v}$, $\boldsymbol{w}$ are non-coplanar. By Theorem 2.5, $\{\boldsymbol{u}, \boldsymbol{v}, \boldsymbol{w}\}$ is a basis for space. Hence

$$\begin{aligned} x\boldsymbol{u}+y\boldsymbol{v}+z\boldsymbol{w} = \boldsymbol{0} &\Rightarrow x\boldsymbol{u}+y\boldsymbol{v}+z\boldsymbol{w} = 0\boldsymbol{u}+0\boldsymbol{v}+0\boldsymbol{w} \\ &\Rightarrow x = 0, y = 0, z = 0, \end{aligned}$$

by the uniqueness of components, and so condition (4.9) is satisfied.

(ii) Suppose now that condition (4.9) is satisfied, and that $\boldsymbol{u}$, $\boldsymbol{v}$, $\boldsymbol{w}$ are coplanar. We can suppose that $\boldsymbol{u}$, $\boldsymbol{v}$ are non-parallel; otherwise $\boldsymbol{v} = p\boldsymbol{u}$ with $p \neq 0$ and so the equation $p\boldsymbol{u}-\boldsymbol{v}+0\boldsymbol{w} = \boldsymbol{0}$ holds, which contradicts (4.9).

By Theorem **2.4**, we can express $\boldsymbol{w}$ as a sum of scalar multiples of $\boldsymbol{u}$, $\boldsymbol{v}$, say $\boldsymbol{w} = x\boldsymbol{u}+y\boldsymbol{v}$. Then $x\boldsymbol{u}+y\boldsymbol{v}+(-1)\boldsymbol{w} = \boldsymbol{0}$. By (4.9), this implies that $x = 0$, $y = 0$, $-1 = 0$, which is impossible. Thus $\boldsymbol{u}$, $\boldsymbol{v}$, $\boldsymbol{w}$ are non-coplanar, and the proof is complete.

Example 7. Show that the vectors $\boldsymbol{u} = \boldsymbol{i}+2\boldsymbol{k}$, $\boldsymbol{v} = -2\boldsymbol{i}+\boldsymbol{j}+3\boldsymbol{k}$, $\boldsymbol{w} = \boldsymbol{i}+\boldsymbol{j}-\boldsymbol{k}$ form a basis for 3-dimensional euclidean space, and find the components of the vector $\boldsymbol{a} = -\boldsymbol{i}+2\boldsymbol{j}+2\boldsymbol{k}$ with respect to this basis.

We show that $\boldsymbol{u}$, $\boldsymbol{v}$, $\boldsymbol{w}$ are linearly independent.

$$x\boldsymbol{u}+y\boldsymbol{v}+z\boldsymbol{w} = \boldsymbol{0}$$

$$\Rightarrow x(\boldsymbol{i}+2\boldsymbol{k})+y(-2\boldsymbol{i}+\boldsymbol{j}+3\boldsymbol{k})+z(\boldsymbol{i}+\boldsymbol{j}-\boldsymbol{k}) = \boldsymbol{0}$$

$$\Rightarrow (x-2y+z)\boldsymbol{i}+(y+z)\boldsymbol{j}+(2x+3y-z)\boldsymbol{k} = \boldsymbol{0}$$

$$\Rightarrow \begin{cases} x-2y+z = 0 \\ y+z = 0 \\ 2x+3y-z = 0 \end{cases} \quad \text{(since } \boldsymbol{i}, \boldsymbol{j}, \boldsymbol{k} \text{ form a basis)}$$

$$\Rightarrow \begin{cases} x-2y+z = 0 \\ y+z = 0 \\ 7y-3z = 0 \end{cases} \Rightarrow \begin{cases} x-2y+z = 0 \\ y+z = 0 \\ 10z = 0 \end{cases} \Rightarrow z = 0,\ y = 0,\ x = 0.$$

Hence $\boldsymbol{u}$. $\boldsymbol{v}$, $\boldsymbol{w}$ form a basis for space. [Note the "echelon" method of solving the linear equations.]

Now $\boldsymbol{a} = x\boldsymbol{u}+y\boldsymbol{v}+z\boldsymbol{w}$, where

$$-\boldsymbol{i}+2\boldsymbol{j}+2\boldsymbol{k} = (x-2y+z)\boldsymbol{i}+(y+z)\boldsymbol{j}+(2x+3y-z)\boldsymbol{k},$$

i.e. $\begin{cases} x-2y+z = -1, \\ y+z = 2 \\ 2x+3y-z = 2 \end{cases}$ i.e. $\begin{cases} x-2y+z = -1, \\ y+z = 2 \\ 7y-3z = 4 \end{cases}$

i.e. $\begin{cases} x-2y+z = -1, \\ y+z = 2 \\ 10z = 10 \end{cases}$ i.e. $\begin{cases} x = 0 \\ y = 1 \\ z = 1. \end{cases}$

Thus $\boldsymbol{a} = 0\boldsymbol{u}+1\boldsymbol{v}+1\boldsymbol{w} = \boldsymbol{v}+\boldsymbol{w}$, and $\boldsymbol{a}$ has components (0, 1, 1) with respect to the basis $\boldsymbol{u}$, $\boldsymbol{v}$, $\boldsymbol{w}$.

5. Scalar product and vector product of vectors

If $\boldsymbol{a}$ and $\boldsymbol{b}$ are non-zero vectors, we take as the **angle between the directions of** $\boldsymbol{a}$ **and** $\boldsymbol{b}$ that angle between them whose measure θ in radians lies in the interval $0 \leqslant \theta \leqslant \pi$.

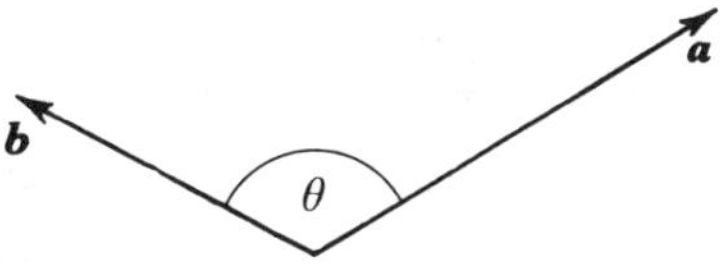

Scalar product. If $\boldsymbol{a} \neq \boldsymbol{0}$ and $\boldsymbol{b} \neq \boldsymbol{0}$, then the **scalar product** of $\boldsymbol{a}$, $\boldsymbol{b}$ is denoted by $\boldsymbol{a}.\boldsymbol{b}$ and defined by writing

$$\boldsymbol{a}.\boldsymbol{b} = |\boldsymbol{a}||\boldsymbol{b}| \cos \theta,$$

where θ is the angle between $\boldsymbol{a}$ and $\boldsymbol{b}$.

If either $\boldsymbol{a} = \boldsymbol{0}$ or $\boldsymbol{b} = \boldsymbol{0}$, then $\boldsymbol{a}.\boldsymbol{b}$ is defined to be the scalar 0.

Some properties of scalar product

(1) If $\boldsymbol{a}$ and $\boldsymbol{b}$ are non-zero and θ is the angle between them, then

$$\cos \theta = \frac{\boldsymbol{a}.\boldsymbol{b}}{|\boldsymbol{a}||\boldsymbol{b}|}.$$

In particular, if $\boldsymbol{a}$, $\boldsymbol{b}$ are *unit vectors*, then $\cos \theta = \boldsymbol{a}.\boldsymbol{b}$.

(2) $\boldsymbol{a}.\boldsymbol{b} = 0 \Leftrightarrow \boldsymbol{a}$ *is perpendicular to* $\boldsymbol{b}$ *or at least one of* $\boldsymbol{a}$, $\boldsymbol{b}$ *is* $\boldsymbol{0}$.

For, $\quad \boldsymbol{a}.\boldsymbol{b} = 0 \Leftrightarrow \cos \theta = 0$ or at least one of $\boldsymbol{a}$, $\boldsymbol{b}$ is $\boldsymbol{0}$

$\Leftrightarrow \theta = \frac{1}{2}\pi$ or at least one of $\boldsymbol{a}$, $\boldsymbol{b}$ is $\boldsymbol{0}$.

(3) $\boldsymbol{a}.\boldsymbol{a} = |\boldsymbol{a}|^2$; for, this is obvious if $\boldsymbol{a} = \boldsymbol{0}$, and, if $\boldsymbol{a} \neq \boldsymbol{0}$,
$\boldsymbol{a}.\boldsymbol{a} = |\boldsymbol{a}||\boldsymbol{a}| \cos 0 = |\boldsymbol{a}|^2$.

The scalar product $\boldsymbol{a}.\boldsymbol{a}$ is often denoted by $\boldsymbol{a}^2$.

(4) $\boldsymbol{a}.\boldsymbol{b} = \boldsymbol{b}.\boldsymbol{a}$; this commutative property is obviously true from the symmetry of the definition of the scalar product.

(5) **Component form of scalar product**: *If* $\boldsymbol{a} = a_1\boldsymbol{i}+a_2\boldsymbol{j}+a_3\boldsymbol{k}$ *and* $\boldsymbol{b} = b_1\boldsymbol{i}+b_2\boldsymbol{j}+b_3\boldsymbol{k}$, *then* $\boldsymbol{a}.\boldsymbol{b} = a_1b_1+a_2b_2+a_3b_3$.

Proof. The result is clearly true if $\boldsymbol{a} = \boldsymbol{0}$ or $\boldsymbol{b} = \boldsymbol{0}$. Suppose then that $\boldsymbol{a} \neq \boldsymbol{0}$, $\boldsymbol{b} \neq \boldsymbol{0}$ and that θ is the angle between $\boldsymbol{a}$ and $\boldsymbol{b}$. If $\overrightarrow{OA} = \boldsymbol{a}$ and $\overrightarrow{OB} = \boldsymbol{b}$, then A has coordinates (a_1, a_2, a_3) and B (b_1, b_2, b_3) with respect to the given coordinate system.

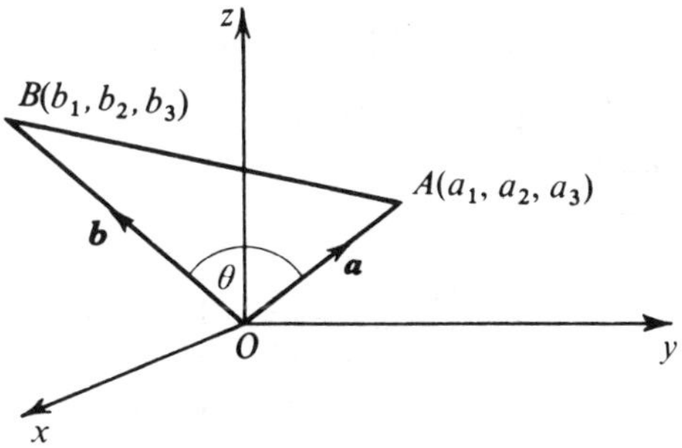

From the cosine formula applied to triangle OAB we have:

$$|AB|^2 = |OA|^2+|OB|^2-2|OA||OB| \cos \theta.$$

Thus

$$(a_1-b_1)^2+(a_2-b_2)^2+(a_3-b_3)^2 = a_1^2+a_2^2+a_3^2+b_1^2+b_2^2+b_3^2-2|\boldsymbol{a}||\boldsymbol{b}|\cos\theta,$$

so that $-2(a_1b_1+a_2b_2+a_3b_3) = -2\boldsymbol{a}.\boldsymbol{b}$, and hence the required result, namely $\boldsymbol{a}.\boldsymbol{b} = a_1b_1+a_2b_2+a_3b_3$, follows.

Note. In the case $\boldsymbol{a} \neq \boldsymbol{0}$, $\boldsymbol{b} \neq \boldsymbol{0}$, it follows that

$$\cos\theta = \frac{a_1b_1+a_2b_2+a_3b_3}{\sqrt{(a_1^2+a_2^2+a_3^2)}\sqrt{(b_1^2+b_2^2+b_3^2)}}.$$

(6) $\boldsymbol{a}.(\boldsymbol{b}+\boldsymbol{c}) = \boldsymbol{a}.\boldsymbol{b}+\boldsymbol{a}.\boldsymbol{c}$, **the distributive property of scalar product.**

Proof. If $\boldsymbol{a} = (a_1, a_2, a_3)$, $\boldsymbol{b} = (b_1, b_2, b_3)$, $\boldsymbol{c} = (c_1, c_2, c_3)$ with respect to the usual $\boldsymbol{i}, \boldsymbol{j}, \boldsymbol{k}$ vectors, then

$$\begin{aligned}\boldsymbol{a}.(\boldsymbol{b}+\boldsymbol{c}) &= (a_1, a_2, a_3).(b_1+c_1, b_2+c_2, b_3+c_3)\\ &= a_1(b_1+c_1)+a_2(b_2+c_2)+a_3(b_3+c_3)\\ &= (a_1b_1+a_2b_2+a_3b_3)+(a_1c_1+a_2c_2+a_3c_3)\\ &= \boldsymbol{a}.\boldsymbol{b}+\boldsymbol{a}.\boldsymbol{c}.\end{aligned}$$

(7) $\boldsymbol{a}.(p\boldsymbol{b}) = p\boldsymbol{a}.\boldsymbol{b} = (p\boldsymbol{a}).\boldsymbol{b}$.

Exercise. Check this result by using components.

(8) $\boldsymbol{i}^2 = \boldsymbol{j}^2 = \boldsymbol{k}^2 = 1$; $\boldsymbol{i}.\boldsymbol{j} = \boldsymbol{j}.\boldsymbol{k} = \boldsymbol{k}.\boldsymbol{i} = 0$. These simply reflect the fact that $\boldsymbol{i}, \boldsymbol{j}, \boldsymbol{k}$ are mutually perpendicular unit vectors. Such a set of vectors is said to form an **orthonormal set of vectors.**

Example 1. A triangle ABC has vertices $A(3, -1, 4)$, $B(2, -2, 1)$ and $C(5, 1, 3)$. Find $\cos\angle BAC$.

$$\overrightarrow{AB} = \boldsymbol{r}_B-\boldsymbol{r}_A = (-1, -1, -3),$$
$$\overrightarrow{AC} = \boldsymbol{r}_C-\boldsymbol{r}_A = (2, 2, -1).$$

$$\cos\angle BAC = \frac{\overrightarrow{AB}.\overrightarrow{AC}}{|AB||AC|} = \frac{-2-2+3}{\sqrt{(11)}\sqrt{(9)}} = \frac{-1}{3\sqrt{(11)}}.$$

Since $\cos\angle BAC$ is negative, $\angle BAC$ is obtuse.

Example 2. Find the two unit vectors which make an angle of $\frac{1}{4}\pi$ radians with the vector $\boldsymbol{i} = (1, 0, 0)$ and are perpendicular to the vector $\boldsymbol{k} = (0, 0, 1)$.

Unit vector $\boldsymbol{u} = (l, m, n)$ satisfies the conditions

$$\Leftrightarrow\ l^2+m^2+n^2 = 1,\quad \boldsymbol{u}.\boldsymbol{i} = \cos\tfrac{1}{4}\pi \text{ and } \boldsymbol{u}.\boldsymbol{k} = 0,$$
$$\Leftrightarrow \begin{cases} l^2+m^2+n^2 = 1 \\ l = 1/\sqrt{2} \\ n = 0 \end{cases} \Leftrightarrow\ l = 1/\sqrt{2},\ m = \pm 1/\sqrt{2},\ n = 0.$$

Thus the two unit vectors are $(1/\sqrt{2}, 1/\sqrt{2}, 0)$ and $(1/\sqrt{2}, -1/\sqrt{2}, 0)$.

Orthogonal projection of non-zero vector $\boldsymbol{b}$ on non-zero vector $\boldsymbol{a}$.

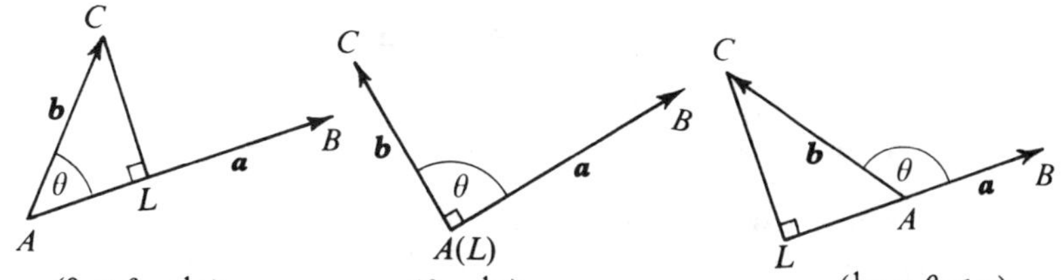

$(0 \leqslant \theta < \frac{1}{2}\pi)$ $(\theta = \frac{1}{2}\pi)$ $(\frac{1}{2}\pi < \theta \leqslant \pi)$

We take $\overrightarrow{AB} = \boldsymbol{a}$, $\overrightarrow{AC} = \boldsymbol{b}$ and denote by L the projection of C on the line AB. If θ is the angle between $\boldsymbol{a}$ and $\boldsymbol{b}$, then $AL/AC = \cos\theta$, and so

$$AL = |\boldsymbol{b}| \cos\theta = |\boldsymbol{b}| \frac{\boldsymbol{a}.\boldsymbol{b}}{|\boldsymbol{a}||\boldsymbol{b}|} = \frac{\boldsymbol{a}.\boldsymbol{b}}{|\boldsymbol{a}|} = \boldsymbol{b}.\frac{\boldsymbol{a}}{|\boldsymbol{a}|} = \boldsymbol{b}.\boldsymbol{u}, \tag{5.1}$$

where $\boldsymbol{u} = \boldsymbol{a}/|\boldsymbol{a}|$ is the unit vector in the direction of $\boldsymbol{a}$.

AL is called the **scalar orthogonal projection** of $\boldsymbol{b}$ on $\boldsymbol{a}$; we note that $\boldsymbol{a}.\boldsymbol{b} = |\boldsymbol{a}|AL$.

The vector

$$\overrightarrow{AL} = AL\boldsymbol{u} = \left(\frac{\boldsymbol{a}.\boldsymbol{b}}{|\boldsymbol{a}|}\right)\frac{\boldsymbol{a}}{|\boldsymbol{a}|} = \frac{\boldsymbol{a}.\boldsymbol{b}}{|\boldsymbol{a}|^2}\boldsymbol{a}$$

is called the **vector orthogonal projection** of $\boldsymbol{b}$ on $\boldsymbol{a}$.

Example 3. If A is the point $(1, 0, 0)$, $B(2, 1, 3)$ and $C(-1, 4, 5)$, find the measure of the orthogonal projection of $\overrightarrow{AC}$ on $\overrightarrow{AB}$.

By (5.1), this measure is $\overrightarrow{AC}.\overrightarrow{AB}/|\overrightarrow{AB}|$.

Now $\overrightarrow{AC} = (-2, 4, 5)$ and $\overrightarrow{AB} = (1, 1, 3)$; thus the required measure is

$$\frac{(-2, 4, 5).(1, 1, 3)}{\sqrt{(1+1+9)}} = \frac{-2+4+15}{\sqrt{(11)}} = \frac{17}{\sqrt{(11)}}.$$

Additive property of orthogonal projections. We prove the following result:

The projection of $\boldsymbol{b}+\boldsymbol{c}$ on $\boldsymbol{a}$ = (the projection of $\boldsymbol{b}$ on $\boldsymbol{a}$)+(the projection of $\boldsymbol{c}$ on $\boldsymbol{a}$).

Proof. We consider scalar projections; the result for vector projections then follows.

The projection of $\boldsymbol{b}+\boldsymbol{c}$ on $\boldsymbol{a} = (\boldsymbol{b}+\boldsymbol{c}).\boldsymbol{u}$, where $\boldsymbol{u} = \boldsymbol{a}/|\boldsymbol{a}|$

$= \boldsymbol{b}.\boldsymbol{u}+\boldsymbol{c}.\boldsymbol{u}$, by property (6) for scalar products. From this, the required result follows since $\boldsymbol{b}.\boldsymbol{u}$ and $\boldsymbol{c}.\boldsymbol{u}$ are respectively the projections of $\boldsymbol{b}$ and $\boldsymbol{c}$ on $\boldsymbol{a}$.

Note. If $\boldsymbol{a} = a_1\boldsymbol{i}+a_2\boldsymbol{j}+a_3\boldsymbol{k}$, then $a_1 = \boldsymbol{a}.\boldsymbol{i}$ = the scalar projection of a on $\boldsymbol{i}$; similarly a_2 and a_3 are the scalar projections of $\boldsymbol{a}$ on $\boldsymbol{j}$ and $\boldsymbol{k}$.

Extension of the additive property of orthogonal projections.

The projection of $(\boldsymbol{b}_1+\boldsymbol{b}_2+\ldots+\boldsymbol{b}_n)$ *on* $\boldsymbol{a} = \sum_{i=1}^{n}$ *(the projection of* $\boldsymbol{b}_i$ on $\boldsymbol{a}$).

Exercise. Write out a proof by induction of this result.

The vector product of the ordered pair of vectors $\boldsymbol{a}$, $\boldsymbol{b}$. We start with two *non-zero, non-parallel* vectors $\boldsymbol{a}$, $\boldsymbol{b}$ and denote by θ $(0<\theta<\pi)$ the angle between them. The **vector product** of the pair $\boldsymbol{a}$, $\boldsymbol{b}$ is denoted by $\boldsymbol{a}\times\boldsymbol{b}$ and is the vector defined as follows:

(1) $|\boldsymbol{a}\times\boldsymbol{b}| = |\boldsymbol{a}||\boldsymbol{b}|\sin\theta$;

(2) the direction of $\boldsymbol{a}\times\boldsymbol{b}$ is perpendicular to the plane of $\boldsymbol{a}$, $\boldsymbol{b}$ and is such that the triple of vectors $\boldsymbol{a}$, $\boldsymbol{b}$, $\boldsymbol{a}\times\boldsymbol{b}$ form a *right-handed* system. [If we take representations from a point A and look in the direction of $\boldsymbol{a}\times\boldsymbol{b}$, from below the plane of $\boldsymbol{a}$ and $\boldsymbol{b}$, $\boldsymbol{a}$ has to be rotated in a clockwise direction to coincide with the line of $\boldsymbol{b}$.]

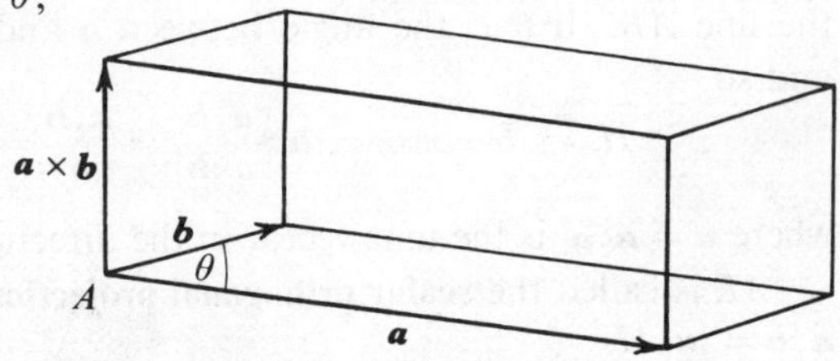

If $\boldsymbol{a}$ is parallel to $\boldsymbol{b}$ or at least one of $\boldsymbol{a}$, $\boldsymbol{b}$ is $\boldsymbol{0}$ we define $\boldsymbol{a}\times\boldsymbol{b}$ to be $\boldsymbol{0}$.

Some properties of vector product

(1) $\boldsymbol{a}\times\boldsymbol{b}=\boldsymbol{0} \Leftrightarrow \boldsymbol{a}$ *is parallel to* $\boldsymbol{b}$ *or at least one of* $\boldsymbol{a}$, $\boldsymbol{b}$ *is* $\boldsymbol{0}$.

This follows at once from the definition; note that $\boldsymbol{a}\times\boldsymbol{a}=\boldsymbol{0}$.

(2) $|\boldsymbol{a}\times\boldsymbol{b}|$ = *the area of the parallelogram with sides determined by the vectors* $\boldsymbol{a}$, $\boldsymbol{b}$.

Proof. Each side of the equation is zero if $\boldsymbol{a}\times\boldsymbol{b}=\boldsymbol{0}$. The non-zero case follows at once from the fact that each side of the equation is then $|\boldsymbol{a}||\boldsymbol{b}|\sin\theta$.

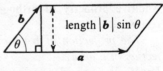

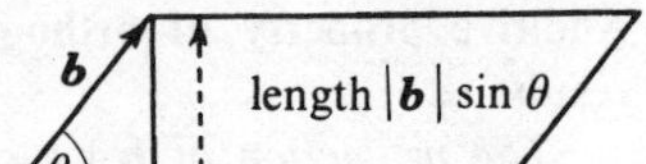

(3) *If* $\boldsymbol{a}\times\boldsymbol{b}\neq\boldsymbol{0}$, *then* $\boldsymbol{u}=\boldsymbol{a}\times\boldsymbol{b}/|\boldsymbol{a}\times\boldsymbol{b}|$ *is a unit vector perpendicular to a plane determined by* $\boldsymbol{a}$ *and* $\boldsymbol{b}$.

This follows at once from the definition of $\boldsymbol{a}\times\boldsymbol{b}$; $-\boldsymbol{u}$ is also a unit vector perpendicular to any plane determined by $\boldsymbol{a}$ and $\boldsymbol{b}$.

(4) $\boldsymbol{b}\times\boldsymbol{a} = -\boldsymbol{a}\times\boldsymbol{b}$. This result is clearly true when $\boldsymbol{a}\times\boldsymbol{b}=\boldsymbol{0}$ and is also true when $\boldsymbol{a}\times\boldsymbol{b}\neq\boldsymbol{0}$ since $\boldsymbol{b}\times\boldsymbol{a}$ has the same magnitude as $\boldsymbol{a}\times\boldsymbol{b}$ but is in the direction opposite to that of $\boldsymbol{a}\times\boldsymbol{b}$.

(5) $\boldsymbol{a}\times(p\boldsymbol{b}) = p\boldsymbol{a}\times\boldsymbol{b} = (p\boldsymbol{a})\times\boldsymbol{b}$ *for any scalar* p.

Exercise. Write out a proof of result (5).

(6) *Geometrical meaning for* $\boldsymbol{a}.\boldsymbol{b}\times\boldsymbol{c}$, *called the* **scalar triple product** *of the vectors* $\boldsymbol{a}$, $\boldsymbol{b}$, $\boldsymbol{c}$. If $\boldsymbol{a}=\boldsymbol{0}$ or $\boldsymbol{b}\times\boldsymbol{c}=\boldsymbol{0}$, then $\boldsymbol{a}.\boldsymbol{b}\times\boldsymbol{c}$ is 0. We now suppose that $\boldsymbol{a}\neq\boldsymbol{0}$ and $\boldsymbol{b}\times\boldsymbol{c}\neq\boldsymbol{0}$, and take $\overrightarrow{AE}=\boldsymbol{a}$, $\overrightarrow{AB}=\boldsymbol{b}$, $\overrightarrow{AD}=\boldsymbol{c}$ and complete the parallelepiped $ABCDEFGH$ indicated.

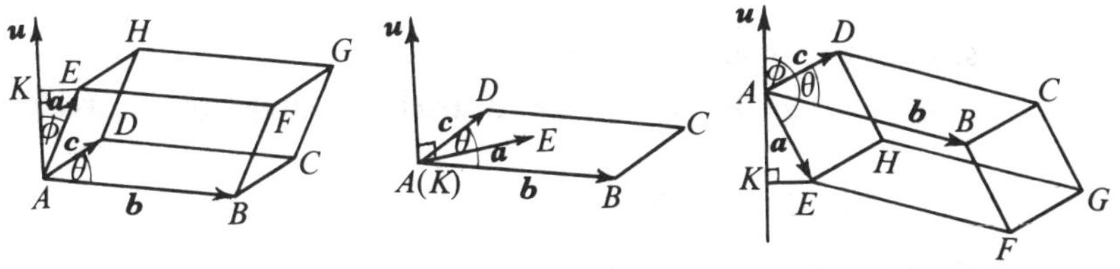

$(0\leqslant\phi<\frac{1}{2}\pi)$ $(\phi=\frac{1}{2}\pi)$ $(\frac{1}{2}\pi<\phi\leqslant\pi)$

If θ is the angle between $\boldsymbol{b}$ and $\boldsymbol{c}$ and ϕ is the angle between $\boldsymbol{a}$ and $\boldsymbol{u}$, where $\boldsymbol{u}=\boldsymbol{b}\times\boldsymbol{c}/|\boldsymbol{b}\times\boldsymbol{c}|$, the unit vector in the direction of $\boldsymbol{b}\times\boldsymbol{c}$, then

$$\begin{aligned}\boldsymbol{a}.\boldsymbol{b}\times\boldsymbol{c} &= |\boldsymbol{b}\times\boldsymbol{c}||\boldsymbol{a}|\cos\phi\\ &= (\text{area of parallelogram } ABCD).AK,\end{aligned}$$

where AK is the scalar projection of $\boldsymbol{a}$ on $\boldsymbol{u}$.
Thus

$\boldsymbol{a}.\boldsymbol{b}\times\boldsymbol{c}=$ (i) 0 if $\phi=\frac{1}{2}\pi$, i.e. if $\boldsymbol{a}$, $\boldsymbol{b}$, $\boldsymbol{c}$ are coplanar,

(ii) a positive number equal to the volume of parallelepiped $ABCDEFGH$ if $\cos\phi>0$, i.e. if $0\leqslant\phi<\frac{1}{2}\pi$, i.e. if the triple of vectors $\boldsymbol{a}$, $\boldsymbol{b}$, $\boldsymbol{c}$ forms a right-handed system,

(iii) a negative number equal in absolute value to the volume of the parallelepiped $ABCDEFGH$ if $\cos\phi<0$, i.e. if $\frac{1}{2}\pi<\phi\leqslant\pi$, i.e. if the vectors $\boldsymbol{a}$, $\boldsymbol{b}$, $\boldsymbol{c}$ form a left-handed system.

We say that $\boldsymbol{a}.\boldsymbol{b}\times\boldsymbol{c}=$ the **signed volume** of the **parallelepiped determined by the ordered triple of vectors** $\boldsymbol{a}$, $\boldsymbol{b}$, $\boldsymbol{c}$.

Notes: 1. $\boldsymbol{a}.\boldsymbol{b}\times\boldsymbol{c}$ is often denoted by $[\boldsymbol{a}, \boldsymbol{b}, \boldsymbol{c}]$.

2. From the above discussion it is clear that vectors $\boldsymbol{a}$, $\boldsymbol{b}$, $\boldsymbol{c}$ are non-coplanar if and only if $[\boldsymbol{a}, \boldsymbol{b}, \boldsymbol{c}]\neq 0$.

3. Since, by cyclic symmetry, the triples of vectors $\{\boldsymbol{a}, \boldsymbol{b}, \boldsymbol{c}\}$, $\{\boldsymbol{b}, \boldsymbol{c}, \boldsymbol{a}\}$ and $\{\boldsymbol{c}, \boldsymbol{a}, \boldsymbol{b}\}$ are either all coplanar sets, or all right-handed systems, or all left-handed systems, we deduce immediately the following important property of scalar triple product:

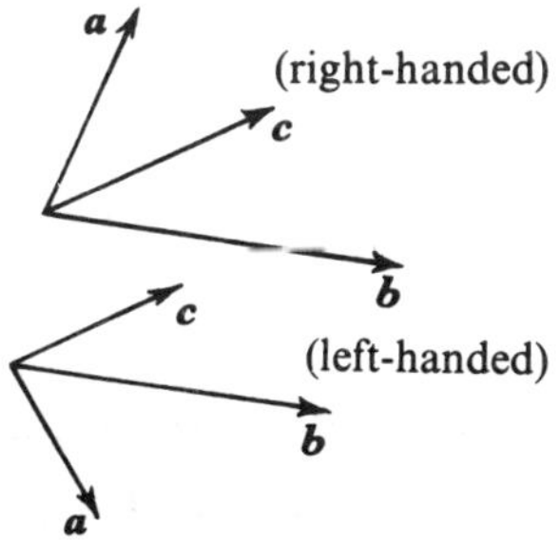

$$[\boldsymbol{a}, \boldsymbol{b}, \boldsymbol{c}]=[\boldsymbol{b}, \boldsymbol{c}, \boldsymbol{a}]=[\boldsymbol{c}, \boldsymbol{a}, \boldsymbol{b}], \quad (5.2)$$

i.e. $\boldsymbol{a}.\boldsymbol{b}\times\boldsymbol{c}=\boldsymbol{b}.\boldsymbol{c}\times\boldsymbol{a}=\boldsymbol{c}.\boldsymbol{a}\times\boldsymbol{b}$.

Also, each of these equals

$$-[\boldsymbol{a}, \boldsymbol{c}, \boldsymbol{b}] = -[\boldsymbol{b}, \boldsymbol{a}, \boldsymbol{c}] = -[\boldsymbol{c}, \boldsymbol{b}, \boldsymbol{a}],$$

since the triple $\{\boldsymbol{a}, \boldsymbol{b}, \boldsymbol{c}\}$ is right-handed if and only if the triple $\{\boldsymbol{a}, \boldsymbol{c}, \boldsymbol{b}\}$ is left-handed, and since the triples are simultaneously coplanar.

We use (5.2) to prove the following result.

(7) $\boldsymbol{a}\times(\boldsymbol{b}+\boldsymbol{c}) = \boldsymbol{a}\times\boldsymbol{b}+\boldsymbol{a}\times\boldsymbol{c}$, **the distributive property of vector product.**

Proof. We consider $\boldsymbol{d} = \boldsymbol{a}\times(\boldsymbol{b}+\boldsymbol{c})-\boldsymbol{a}\times\boldsymbol{b}-\boldsymbol{a}\times\boldsymbol{c}$. We have:

$\boldsymbol{d}^2 = \boldsymbol{d}.[\boldsymbol{a}\times(\boldsymbol{b}+\boldsymbol{c})-\boldsymbol{a}\times\boldsymbol{b}-\boldsymbol{a}\times\boldsymbol{c}]$

$= \boldsymbol{d}.\boldsymbol{a}\times(\boldsymbol{b}+\boldsymbol{c})-\boldsymbol{d}.\boldsymbol{a}\times\boldsymbol{b}-\boldsymbol{d}.\boldsymbol{a}\times\boldsymbol{c}$, by the distributive property for scalar product,

$= (\boldsymbol{b}+\boldsymbol{c}).\boldsymbol{d}\times\boldsymbol{a}-\boldsymbol{d}.\boldsymbol{a}\times\boldsymbol{b}-\boldsymbol{d}.\boldsymbol{a}\times\boldsymbol{c}$, applying (5.2) to the first term,

$= \boldsymbol{b}.\boldsymbol{d}\times\boldsymbol{a}+\boldsymbol{c}.\boldsymbol{d}\times\boldsymbol{a}-\boldsymbol{d}.\boldsymbol{a}\times\boldsymbol{b}-\boldsymbol{d}.\boldsymbol{a}\times\boldsymbol{c}$, by the distributive property for scalar product,

$= \boldsymbol{d}.\boldsymbol{a}\times\boldsymbol{b}+\boldsymbol{d}.\boldsymbol{a}\times\boldsymbol{c}-\boldsymbol{d}.\boldsymbol{a}\times\boldsymbol{b}-\boldsymbol{d}.\boldsymbol{a}\times\boldsymbol{c}$, applying (5.2) to the first two terms,

$= 0.$

Hence $\boldsymbol{d} = \boldsymbol{0}$, and the required result follows.

(8) **The components of $\boldsymbol{a}\times\boldsymbol{b}$ with respect to the coordinate vectors $\boldsymbol{i}, \boldsymbol{j}, \boldsymbol{k}$.**

We note that $\boldsymbol{i}\times\boldsymbol{i} = \boldsymbol{0}$, $\boldsymbol{j}\times\boldsymbol{j} = \boldsymbol{0}$, $\boldsymbol{k}\times\boldsymbol{k} = \boldsymbol{0}$.

Also,

$$|\boldsymbol{i}\times\boldsymbol{j}| = |\boldsymbol{i}||\boldsymbol{j}| \sin \tfrac{1}{2}\pi = 1,$$

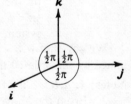

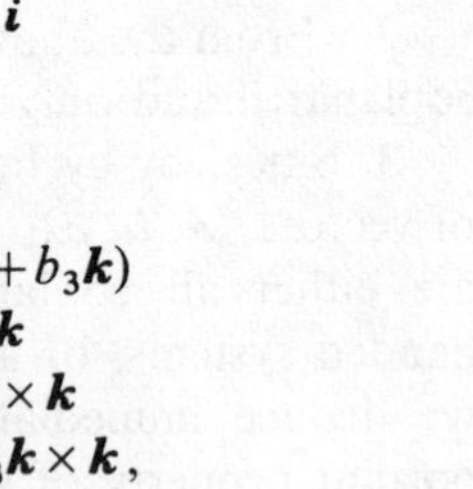

so that $\boldsymbol{i}\times\boldsymbol{j}$ is a unit vector forming a right-handed set with $\boldsymbol{i}, \boldsymbol{j}$. Hence $\boldsymbol{i}\times\boldsymbol{j} = \boldsymbol{k} = -\boldsymbol{j}\times\boldsymbol{i}$; similarly

$$\boldsymbol{j}\times\boldsymbol{k} = \boldsymbol{i} = -\boldsymbol{k}\times\boldsymbol{j}$$

and

$$\boldsymbol{k}\times\boldsymbol{i} = \boldsymbol{j} = -\boldsymbol{i}\times\boldsymbol{k}.$$

If $\boldsymbol{a} = a_1\boldsymbol{i}+a_2\boldsymbol{j}+a_3\boldsymbol{k}$ and $\boldsymbol{b} = b_1\boldsymbol{i}+b_2\boldsymbol{j}+b_3\boldsymbol{k}$, then

$$\begin{aligned}\boldsymbol{a}\times\boldsymbol{b} &= (a_1\boldsymbol{i}+a_2\boldsymbol{j}+a_3\boldsymbol{k})\times(b_1\boldsymbol{i}+b_2\boldsymbol{j}+b_3\boldsymbol{k})\\ &= a_1b_1\boldsymbol{i}\times\boldsymbol{i}+a_1b_2\boldsymbol{i}\times\boldsymbol{j}+a_1b_3\boldsymbol{i}\times\boldsymbol{k}\\ &\quad+a_2b_1\boldsymbol{j}\times\boldsymbol{i}+a_2b_2\boldsymbol{j}\times\boldsymbol{j}+a_2b_3\boldsymbol{j}\times\boldsymbol{k}\\ &\quad+a_3b_1\boldsymbol{k}\times\boldsymbol{i}+a_3b_2\boldsymbol{k}\times\boldsymbol{j}+a_3b_3\boldsymbol{k}\times\boldsymbol{k},\end{aligned}$$

by the distributive property of vector products, and so

$$\boldsymbol{a}\times\boldsymbol{b} = (a_2b_3-a_3b_2)\boldsymbol{i}+(a_3b_1-a_1b_3)\boldsymbol{j}+(a_1b_2-a_2b_1)\boldsymbol{k}. \tag{5.3}$$

In 2×2 determinant notation, (5.3) can be written in the form

$$\boldsymbol{a}\times\boldsymbol{b} = \begin{vmatrix} a_2 & a_3 \\ b_2 & b_3 \end{vmatrix}\boldsymbol{i}+\begin{vmatrix} a_3 & a_1 \\ b_3 & b_1 \end{vmatrix}\boldsymbol{j}+\begin{vmatrix} a_1 & a_2 \\ b_1 & b_2 \end{vmatrix}\boldsymbol{k}.$$

It is often convenient to use the 3×3 determinant notation

$$\boldsymbol{a}\times\boldsymbol{b} = \begin{vmatrix} \boldsymbol{i} & \boldsymbol{j} & \boldsymbol{k} \\ a_1 & a_2 & a_3 \\ b_1 & b_2 & b_3 \end{vmatrix}$$

Component form of the scalar triple product $[\boldsymbol{a}, \boldsymbol{b}, \boldsymbol{c}]$. If

$$\boldsymbol{a} = a_1\boldsymbol{i}+a_2\boldsymbol{j}+a_3\boldsymbol{k},\quad \boldsymbol{b} = b_1\boldsymbol{i}+b_2\boldsymbol{j}+b_3\boldsymbol{k}\quad\text{and}\quad \boldsymbol{c} = c_1\boldsymbol{i}+c_2\boldsymbol{j}+c_3\boldsymbol{k},$$

then

$$[\boldsymbol{a}, \boldsymbol{b}, \boldsymbol{c}] = \boldsymbol{a}.\boldsymbol{b}\times\boldsymbol{c} = a_1(b_2c_3-b_3c_2)+a_2(b_3c_1-b_1c_3)+a_3(b_1c_2-b_2c_1)$$

$$= \begin{vmatrix} a_1 & a_2 & a_3 \\ b_1 & b_2 & b_3 \\ c_1 & c_2 & c_3 \end{vmatrix},$$

in 3×3 determinant notation.

Properties of $[\boldsymbol{a}, \boldsymbol{b}, \boldsymbol{c}]$ can be deduced from properties of 3×3 determinants.

(9) **Vector triple product; $\boldsymbol{a}\times(\boldsymbol{b}\times\boldsymbol{c}) = (\boldsymbol{a}.\boldsymbol{c})\boldsymbol{b}-(\boldsymbol{a}.\boldsymbol{b})\boldsymbol{c}$.** (5.4)

Proof. If $\boldsymbol{a} = a_1\boldsymbol{i}+a_2\boldsymbol{j}+a_3\boldsymbol{k}$, $\boldsymbol{b} = b_1\boldsymbol{i}+b_2\boldsymbol{j}+b_3\boldsymbol{k}$, $\boldsymbol{c} = c_1\boldsymbol{i}+c_2\boldsymbol{j}+c_3\boldsymbol{k}$, then

$$\boldsymbol{a}\times(\boldsymbol{b}\times\boldsymbol{c}) = (a_1\boldsymbol{i}+a_2\boldsymbol{j}+a_3\boldsymbol{k})\times\{(b_2c_3-b_3c_2)\boldsymbol{i}+(b_3c_1-b_1c_3)\boldsymbol{j}+$$
$$+(b_1c_2-b_2c_1)\boldsymbol{k}\}$$
$$= [a_2(b_1c_2-b_2c_1)-a_3(b_3c_1-b_1c_3)]\boldsymbol{i}+[\ldots]\boldsymbol{j}+[\ldots]\boldsymbol{k}$$
$$= [(a_1c_1+a_2c_2+a_3c_3)b_1-(a_1b_1+a_2b_2+a_3b_3)c_1]\boldsymbol{i}+[\ldots]\boldsymbol{j}+[\ldots]\boldsymbol{k}$$
$$= (\boldsymbol{a}.\boldsymbol{c})(b_1\boldsymbol{i}+b_2\boldsymbol{j}+b_3\boldsymbol{k})-(\boldsymbol{a}.\boldsymbol{b})(c_1\boldsymbol{i}+c_2\boldsymbol{j}+c_3\boldsymbol{k})$$
$$= (\boldsymbol{a}.\boldsymbol{c})\boldsymbol{b}-(\boldsymbol{a}.\boldsymbol{b})\boldsymbol{c}.$$

Example 4. Find the unit vectors perpendicular to both of the vectors $\boldsymbol{a} = 2\boldsymbol{i}+\boldsymbol{j}-\boldsymbol{k}$ and $\boldsymbol{b} = \boldsymbol{i}+3\boldsymbol{j}-2\boldsymbol{k}$.

The required vectors are $\pm(\boldsymbol{a}\times\boldsymbol{b})/(|\boldsymbol{a}\times\boldsymbol{b}|)$.

Now $$\boldsymbol{a}\times\boldsymbol{b} = \begin{vmatrix} \boldsymbol{i} & \boldsymbol{j} & \boldsymbol{k} \\ 2 & 1 & -1 \\ 1 & 3 & -2 \end{vmatrix} = \boldsymbol{i}+3\boldsymbol{j}+5\boldsymbol{k};\quad |\boldsymbol{a}\times\boldsymbol{b}| = \sqrt{(35)}.$$

Thus the unit vectors are $\pm\dfrac{1}{\sqrt{(35)}}(\boldsymbol{i}+3\boldsymbol{j}+5\boldsymbol{k})$.

Example 5. If $\boldsymbol{a} \neq \boldsymbol{0}$, and if $\boldsymbol{a}.\boldsymbol{b} = \boldsymbol{a}.\boldsymbol{c}$ and $\boldsymbol{a}\times\boldsymbol{b} = \boldsymbol{a}\times\boldsymbol{c}$, show that $\boldsymbol{b} = \boldsymbol{c}$.

We have (noting that $\boldsymbol{a} \neq \boldsymbol{0}$):

$\boldsymbol{a}.(\boldsymbol{b}-\boldsymbol{c}) = 0$, so either $\boldsymbol{b}-\boldsymbol{c} = \boldsymbol{0}$ or $\boldsymbol{b}-\boldsymbol{c}$ is perpendicular to $\boldsymbol{a}$;
$\boldsymbol{a}\times(\boldsymbol{b}-\boldsymbol{c}) = \boldsymbol{0}$, so either $\boldsymbol{b}-\boldsymbol{c} = \boldsymbol{0}$ or $\boldsymbol{b}-\boldsymbol{c}$ is parallel to $\boldsymbol{a}$.

Hence the only possibility is $\boldsymbol{b}-\boldsymbol{c} = \boldsymbol{0}$, i.e. $\boldsymbol{b} = \boldsymbol{c}$.

Example 6. Show that $(\boldsymbol{a}\times\boldsymbol{b}).(\boldsymbol{c}\times\boldsymbol{d}) = (\boldsymbol{a}.\boldsymbol{c})(\boldsymbol{b}.\boldsymbol{d})-(\boldsymbol{a}.\boldsymbol{d})(\boldsymbol{b}.\boldsymbol{c})$.

$$\begin{aligned}(\boldsymbol{a}\times\boldsymbol{b}).(\boldsymbol{c}\times\boldsymbol{d}) &= (\boldsymbol{c}\times\boldsymbol{d}).(\boldsymbol{a}\times\boldsymbol{b}) \\ &= [\boldsymbol{c}\times\boldsymbol{d}, \boldsymbol{a}, \boldsymbol{b}] \\ &= [\boldsymbol{a}, \boldsymbol{b}, \boldsymbol{c}\times\boldsymbol{d}] &&\text{, by (5.2),} \\ &= \boldsymbol{a}.\big(\boldsymbol{b}\times(\boldsymbol{c}\times\boldsymbol{d})\big) \\ &= \boldsymbol{a}.\{(\boldsymbol{b}.\boldsymbol{d})\boldsymbol{c}-(\boldsymbol{b}.\boldsymbol{c})\boldsymbol{d}\} &&\text{, using (5.4),} \\ &= (\boldsymbol{a}.\boldsymbol{c})(\boldsymbol{b}.\boldsymbol{d})-(\boldsymbol{a}.\boldsymbol{d})(\boldsymbol{b}.\boldsymbol{c}).\end{aligned}$$

6. Applications in geometry of scalar and vector products

A non-zero vector is said to be a **normal vector** to a given plane if its direction is perpendicular to the plane.

Scalar equation of the plane through the point $A(\boldsymbol{a})$ with a normal direction given by the unit vector $\boldsymbol{u}$.

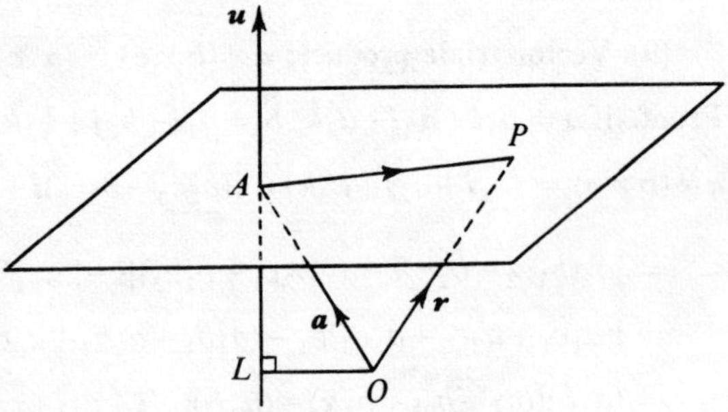

As usual we denote by $\boldsymbol{r}$ the position vector of a point P.

The set of points on the plane

$= \{A\}\cup\{P : \overrightarrow{AP}$ perpendicular to $\boldsymbol{u}\}$
$= \{A\}\cup\{P : \overrightarrow{AP}.\boldsymbol{u}=0\}$
$= \{\boldsymbol{r} : (\boldsymbol{r}-\boldsymbol{a}).\boldsymbol{u}=0\}$,

since $\boldsymbol{r} = \boldsymbol{a}$ gives the point A.

Hence the plane has equation

$$(\boldsymbol{r}-\boldsymbol{a}).\boldsymbol{u} = 0. \tag{6.1}$$

Equation (6.1) can be written in the form:

$$\boldsymbol{r}.\boldsymbol{u} = \boldsymbol{a}.\boldsymbol{u} = LA \quad \text{(a constant)}, \tag{6.2}$$

the scalar projection of $\boldsymbol{a}$ on $\boldsymbol{u}$; LA is often called the signed distance of the plane from O, relative to the normal direction $\boldsymbol{u}$.

Coordinate form of equation (6.1). If $\boldsymbol{a} = (x_1, y_1, z_1)$, $\boldsymbol{u} = (l, m, n)$ and $\boldsymbol{r} = (x, y, z)$, then equation (6.1) can be written as:

$$l(x-x_1)+m(y-y_1)+n(z-z_1) = 0, \tag{6.3}$$

i.e.

$$lx+my+nz = lx_1+my_1+nz_1. \tag{6.4}$$

Note. Since equation (6.3) is homogeneous in l, m, n, the same equation, in which l, m, n are *direction numbers* for a normal direction to the plane and *not direction cosines*, represents the plane. Equation (6.3) (and (6.4)) is of the form $ax+by+cz+d = 0$ with a, b, c, d constants and a, b, c not all zero; a, b, c are direction numbers of a normal direction to the plane. We now prove the converse of this result.

The linear equation $ax+by+cz+d = 0$, *with a, b, c, d constants and a, b, c not all zero, represents a plane for which a, b, c are direction numbers for a normal direction.*

Proof. The equation $ax+by+cz+d = 0$ can be written as

$$\frac{a}{\sqrt{(a^2+b^2+c^2)}}x+\frac{b}{\sqrt{(a^2+b^2+c^2)}}y+\frac{c}{\sqrt{(a^2+b^2+c^2)}}z = \frac{-d}{\sqrt{(a^2+b^2+c^2)}}, \tag{6.5}$$

i.e. $\qquad lx+my+nz = p, \quad$ say,

i.e.

$$\boldsymbol{r}.\boldsymbol{u} = p, \tag{6.6}$$

where $\boldsymbol{u}$ is the unit vector (l, m, n). Hence, by (6.2), the equation represents the plane with $\boldsymbol{u}$ as a unit normal vector and at signed distance $p = (-d)/\sqrt{(a^2+b^2+c^2)}$ from the origin O.

Example 1. Find the (scalar) equation of the plane through the points $A(0, 1, 1)$, $B(1, 2, 0)$, $C(1, 3, 0)$.

A normal direction to the plane is that of $\overrightarrow{AB}\times\overrightarrow{AC}$.

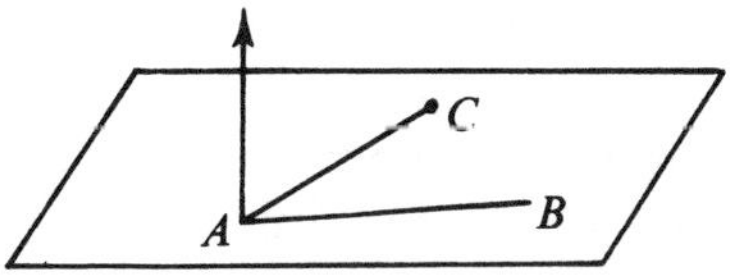

Now $\overrightarrow{AB} = (1, 1, -1)$,

and $\overrightarrow{AC} = (1, 2, -1)$,

so that $\overrightarrow{AB}\times\overrightarrow{AC} = (1, 0, 1)$.

Thus the plane has equation $1x+0y+1z = k$ (k constant), where, since $A \in$ the plane, $1.0+0.1+1.1 = k$, so that $k = 1$. Hence the plane has equation $x+z = 1$.

We now prove the following result:

The perpendicular distance from the point $A(x_1, y_1, z_1)$ to the plane $ax+by+cz+d = 0$ is

$$\frac{|ax_1+by_1+cz_1+d|}{\sqrt{(a^2+b^2+c^2)}}.$$

Proof. We can rewrite the equation of the plane in the form $\boldsymbol{r}.\boldsymbol{u} = p$, as described in (6.5) and (6.6), with $\boldsymbol{u}$ a unit normal vector

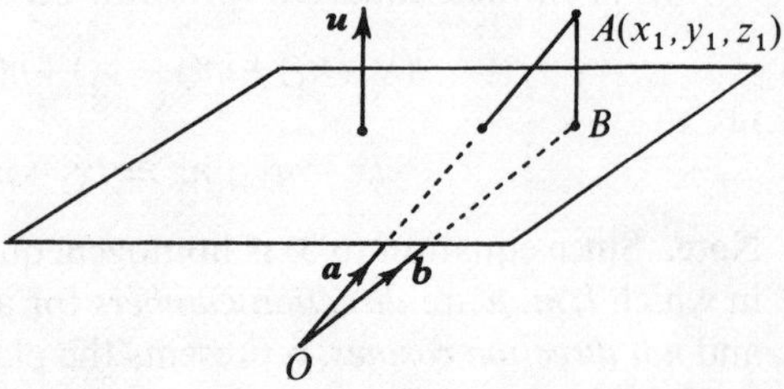

$$\left(\frac{a, b, c}{\sqrt{(a^2+b^2+c^2)}}\right),$$

$$p = \frac{-d}{\sqrt{(a^2+b^2+c^2)}},$$

and $\boldsymbol{r} = (x, y, z)$.

We write $\boldsymbol{a} = (x_1, y_1, z_1)$ and denote by $B(\boldsymbol{b})$ the projection of A on the plane. Since $B \in$ the plane, $\boldsymbol{b}.\boldsymbol{u} = p$.

The required distance $= |AB|$

$$\begin{aligned} &= |\text{the projection of } \overrightarrow{BA} \text{ on unit vector } \boldsymbol{u}| \\ &= |(\boldsymbol{a}-\boldsymbol{b}).\boldsymbol{u}| \\ &= |\boldsymbol{a}.\boldsymbol{u}-p| \\ &= \left|\frac{ax_1+by_1+cz_1}{\sqrt{(a^2+b^2+c^2)}} - \frac{(-d)}{\sqrt{(a^2+b^2+c^2)}}\right| \\ &= \frac{|ax_1+by_1+cz_1+d|}{\sqrt{(a^2+b^2+c^2)}}. \end{aligned}$$

Example 2. Find the equations of the two planes which are perpendicular to the line

$$\frac{(x-1)}{2} = \frac{y}{-1} = \frac{(z+1)}{2}$$

and touch the sphere $x^2+y^2+z^2 = 25$.

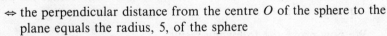

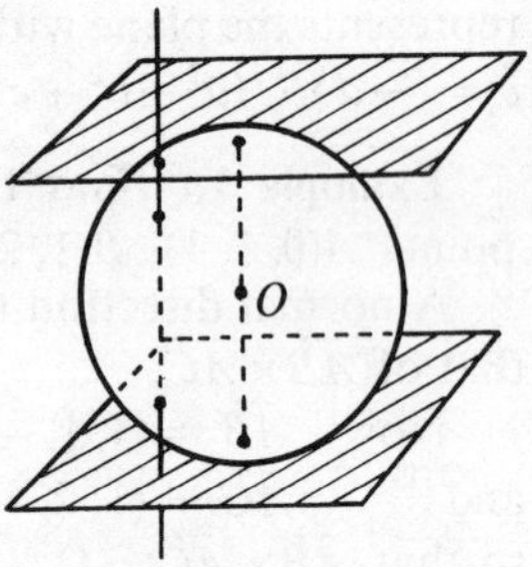

Any plane perpendicular to the given line has a normal direction given by the direction numbers 2, -1, 2, and so has equation of the form

$$2x-y+2z+d = 0, \quad \text{for some } d.$$

This plane touches the sphere

$\Leftrightarrow$ the perpendicular distance from the centre O of the sphere to the plane equals the radius, 5, of the sphere

$$\Leftrightarrow \frac{|d|}{\sqrt{(4+1+4)}} = 5 \Leftrightarrow d = \pm 15.$$

Hence the required planes have equations $2x-y+2z+15 = 0$, and $2x-y+2z-15 = 0$.

7. Worked examples on lines and planes

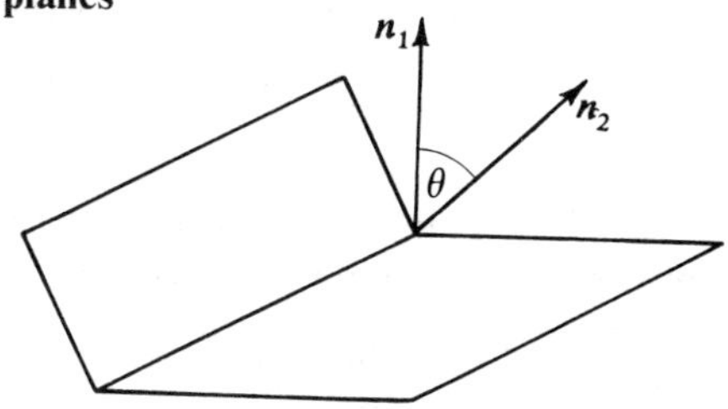

I. An angle between two planes. If $\boldsymbol{n}_1$, $\boldsymbol{n}_2$ are normal vectors to the two planes, then the angle θ between $\boldsymbol{n}_1$ and $\boldsymbol{n}_2$ is called an angle between the two planes. There is a unique angle θ between the two planes satisfying $0 \leqslant \theta \leqslant \frac{1}{2}\pi$.

Example 1. Find the acute angle between the planes $x-2y+z=0$ and $x-y=1$.

The planes have normal directions given by the direction numbers $(1, -2, 1)$ and $(1, -1, 0)$ respectively. If θ is the angle between these directions,

$$\cos\theta = \frac{1.1+(-2).(-1)+1.0}{\sqrt{(1+4+1)}\sqrt{(1+1+0)}} = \frac{3}{\sqrt{6}\sqrt{2}} = \frac{1}{2}\sqrt{3}.$$

Thus $\theta = (1/6)\pi$, and this, since it is acute, is the required angle.

II. Line of intersection of two planes

Example 2. Find equations in symmetric form for the line of intersection of the planes

$$x-y+3z = 2, \tag{7.1}$$

$$3x+y+z = 2. \tag{7.2}$$

We require (i) a direction vector for the line, and (ii) a point on the line.

(i) A direction vector for the line is perpendicular to $\boldsymbol{a} = (1, -1, 3)$, a normal vector to plane (7.1), and also perpendicular to $\boldsymbol{b} = (3, 1, 1)$, a normal vector to plane (7.2). Thus it is parallel to $\boldsymbol{a} \times \boldsymbol{b} = (-4, 8, 4) = 4(-1, 2, 1)$. Hence a direction vector for the line is $(-1, 2, 1)$.

(ii) To find a point on the line it is convenient to find a point on one of the coordinate planes which lies on the line.

To find a point of intersection with the plane $z = 0$ (if such a point exists) we can solve the equations in x, y obtained from (7.1) and (7.2) by taking $z = 0$, namely:

$$\begin{cases} x-y = 2, \\ 3x+y = 2, \end{cases} \quad \text{which give} \quad x = 1,\ y = -1.$$

It follows that the point $(1, -1, 0)$ lies on the line.

From (i) and (ii), symmetric equations for the line are

$$\frac{x-1}{-1} = \frac{y+1}{2} = \frac{z}{1} \quad (= t).$$

Note. If the line does not meet the plane $z = 0$, we can obtain a point on the line by taking $x = 0$ or $y = 0$ in (7.1) and (7.2).

Exercise. Find equations in symmetric form for the line of intersection of the planes $x+y-2z = 2$, $x-2z = 3$.

[In this case, a direction vector for the line is (2, 0, 1), and the point (3, −1, 0) lies on the line. Symmetric equations for the line are

$$\frac{x-3}{2} = \frac{y+1}{0} = \frac{z}{1}, \quad \text{which are often written as:} \quad \frac{x-3}{2} = \frac{z}{1},\ y+1 = 0.$$

III. Projection of a line on a plane

Example 3. Find equations for the projection of the line L with symmetric equations

$$\frac{x-1}{1} = \frac{y}{2} = \frac{z-3}{1}$$

on the plane π with equation $x-2y+3z = 3$.

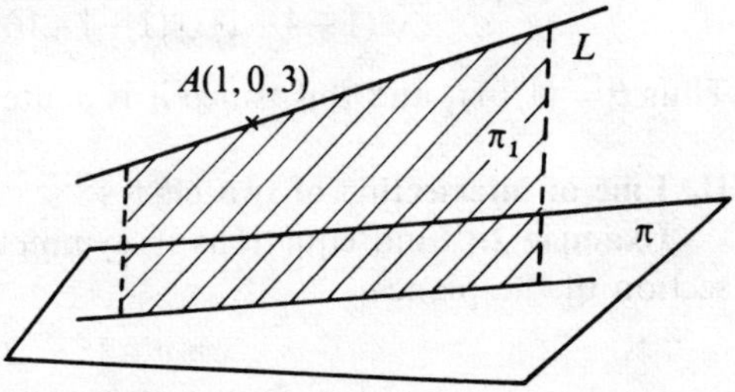

We first find an equation for the plane π_1 which passes through the line L and is perpendicular to the plane π.

A normal vector to π_1 is perpendicular to vector $\boldsymbol{a} = (1, 2, 1)$, a direction vector for L, and is perpendicular to vector $\boldsymbol{b} = (1, -2, 3)$, a normal vector for π. Hence a normal vector to π_1 is parallel to the vector $\boldsymbol{a} \times \boldsymbol{b} = (8, -2, -4) = 2(4, -1, -2)$.

Since the point A (1, 0, 3) lies on L, A is a point on π_1.

Thus π_1 has equation $4x-y-2z = 4.1-0-2.3 = -2$, and equations for the projection of L on π are

$$\begin{cases} x-2y+3z = 3, \\ 4x-y-2z = -2. \end{cases}$$

Exercise. Find equations in symmetric form for this line.

IV. Intersection of line and plane

Example 4. Find the coordinates of the projection Q of the point $P(-3, 2, 6)$ on the plane π with equation $2x-3y-z = 10$.

Since the line PQ is normal to the plane π, PQ is parallel to the vector $(2, -3, -1)$, a normal vector for π. It follows that the line PQ has parametric equations given by $(x, y, z) = (-3, 2, 6) + t(2, -3, -1)$, $(t \in \mathbf{R})$, and so by $x = -3+2t$, $y = 2-3t$, $z = 6-t$.

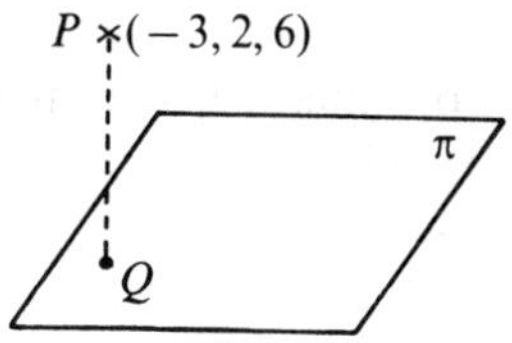

Since $Q \in \pi$, the parameter t of Q is given by

$$2(-3+2t)-3(2-3t)-(6-t) = 10,$$

and so, by $-18+14t = 10$; thus $t = 2$, and Q is the point $(1, -4, 4)$.

V. Coplanar lines. Lines which are coplanar are either parallel (when they do not intersect) or intersecting. In fact, two distinct lines are coplanar if and only if they are either parallel or intersecting (at a unique point).

Example 5. Show that the lines

$$\frac{x-1}{2} = \frac{y-2}{3} = \frac{z-3}{4} (= s), \tag{7.3}$$

and

$$\frac{x-2}{3} = \frac{y-3}{4} = \frac{z-4}{5} (= t) \tag{7.4}$$

are coplanar, and find an equation for the plane containing them.

Since the lines are not parallel, they are coplanar if and only if they have a point in common.

A point on line (7.3) has coordinates $(1+2s, 2+3s, 3+4s)$ for some $s \in \mathbf{R}$, and a point on line (7.4) has coordinates $(2+3t, 3+4t, 4+5t)$ for some $t \in \mathbf{R}$. Consequently the lines are coplanar $\Leftrightarrow \exists s, t \in \mathbf{R}$ such that

$$\begin{cases} 1+2s = 2+3t, \\ 2+3s = 3+4t, \\ 3+4s = 4+5t. \end{cases}$$

On solving the first two of these equations, we obtain $s = -1$, $t = -1$. Since these values of s, t satisfy the third equation also, it follows that the lines meet at the point $(-1, -1, -1)$ and so are coplanar.

A normal vector of the plane determined by the lines is perpendicular to direction vectors of both lines, and so perpendicular to $\boldsymbol{a} = (2, 3, 4)$ and to $\boldsymbol{b} = (3, 4, 5)$. Hence it is parallel to the vector $\boldsymbol{a} \times \boldsymbol{b} = (-1, 2, -1)$. Thus the plane has equation $x-2y+z = (-1)-2.(-1)+(-1) = 0$.

VI. Shortest distance between two non-intersecting lines. If the lines are parallel, the shortest distance between them is clearly the length of any line-segment, with an end point on each line, which is perpendicular to both lines. If the lines are not parallel, they are called **skew lines.**

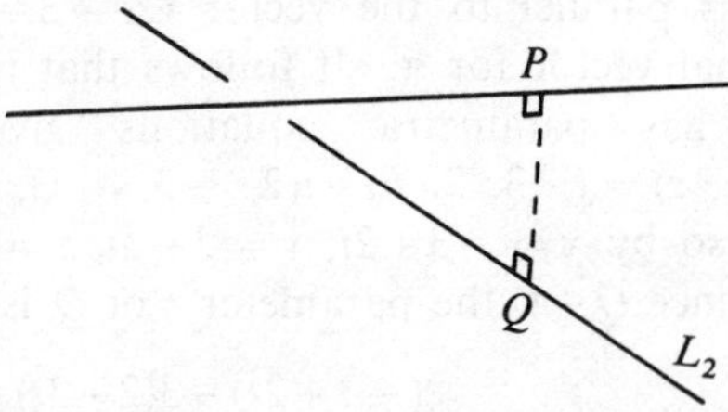

Suppose that L_1, L_2 are skew lines and that $P \in L_1$ and $Q \in L_2$ are such that $|PQ|$ is the shortest distance between the lines. Then the line PQ is perpendicular to both L_1 and L_2. [This follows from the fact that the perpendicular distance from any point Q of L_2 to L_1 is the shortest distance from Q to L_1, and similarly for the shortest distance to L_2 from any point on L_1.] The line-segment $\overrightarrow{PQ}$ (or $\overrightarrow{QP}$) is called their *common perpendicular*.

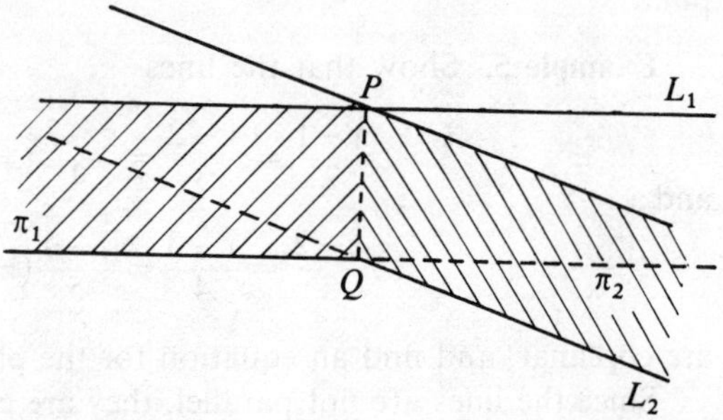

The existence of the common perpendicular of two skew lines L_1, L_2 can be established by noting that the line of intersection of the following two planes π_1, π_2 is perpendicular to L_1 and to L_2 and meets both lines. If $\boldsymbol{a}, \boldsymbol{b}$ are direction vectors for L_1 and L_2, respectively, then π_1 is the plane through L_1 and containing the vector $\boldsymbol{a} \times \boldsymbol{b}$, and π_2 is the plane through L_2 and containing the vector $\boldsymbol{a} \times \boldsymbol{b}$.

Example 6. Find the length of, and equations in symmetric form for, the shortest distance between the lines

$$L_1 : \frac{x-1}{1} = \frac{y-9}{-2} = \frac{z-5}{1} (= s)$$

and

$$L_2 : \frac{x-6}{7} = \frac{y+7}{-6} = \frac{z}{1} (= t),$$

and the coordinates of the points at which it meets L_1 and L_2.

If P is a point of L_1, then its coordinates are of the form $(1+s, 9-2s, 5+s)$ for some $s \in \mathbf{R}$; similarly any point Q of L_2 has coordinates $(6+7t, -7-6t, t)$ for some $t \in \mathbf{R}$.

$$\overrightarrow{PQ} = (5-s+7t, -16+2s-6t, -5-s+t).$$

$\overrightarrow{PQ}$ is perpendicular to the direction vector $\boldsymbol{a} = (1, -2, 1)$ of L_1
$\Leftrightarrow \overrightarrow{PQ}.(1, -2, 1) = 0 \Leftrightarrow (5-s+7t)-2(-16+2s-6t)+(-5-s+t) = 0$
$\Leftrightarrow 3s-10t = 16.$ (7.5)

Also $\overrightarrow{PQ}$ is perpendicular to the direction vector $\boldsymbol{b} = (7, -6, 1)$ of L_2
$\Leftrightarrow \overrightarrow{PQ}.(7, -6, 1) = 0 \Leftrightarrow 7(5-s+7t)-6(-16+2s-6t)+(-5-s+t) = 0$
$\Leftrightarrow 10s-43t = 63.$ (7.6)

On solving (7.5) and (7.6), we obtain $s = 2$ and $t = -1$. Thus the end points of the common perpendicular (i.e. shortest distance) of L_1, L_2 are $P(3, 5, 7)$ on L_1 and $Q(-1, -1, -1)$ on L_2. The length of the shortest distance is $|PQ| = 2\sqrt{(29)}$, and equations for the line PQ are

$$\frac{x+1}{2} = \frac{y+1}{3} = \frac{z+1}{4},$$

noting that $s = 2$, $t = -1$ give $\overrightarrow{PQ} = (-4, -6, -8) = (-2)(2, 3, 4)$.

8. Coordinate systems

The following two sets of coordinates are related to x, y, z-coordinates just as polar coordinates in the plane are related to x, y-coordinates.

(1) Cylindrical polar coordinates (ρ, ϕ, z). We start with the usual axes Ox, Oy, Oz and let $P(x, y, z)$ be a point not on the z-axis. If H, L, M, N are the projections of P on the x, y-plane, the x-axis, the y-axis and the z-axis respectively, we write:

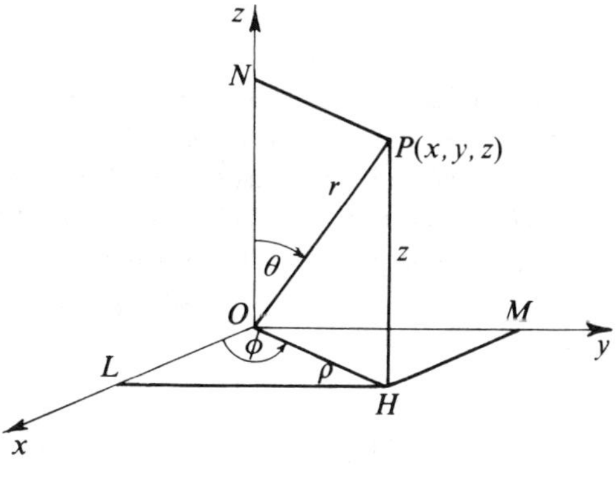

$\angle xOH = \phi$, $0 \leqslant \phi < 2\pi$, $\rho = |OH|$ and $z = ON(= HP)$, (as usual).

Then (ρ, ϕ, z) are called the **cylindrical polar coordinates of** P.

$x = OL = \rho \cos \phi$, $y = OM = \rho \sin \phi$, and $x^2+y^2 = \rho^2$, so that $\rho = \sqrt{(x^2+y^2)}$.

(2) Spherical polar coordinates (r, θ, ϕ). Using the same figure, we write, for a point $P(x, y, z)$ not on the z-axis: $\angle zOP = \theta$, $0 < \theta < \pi$, and

$r = |OP|$. Then (r, θ, ϕ) are called the **spherical polar coordinates of** P. Since $|OH| = r \sin \theta$, we have:

$$x = |OH| \cos \phi = r \sin \theta \cos \phi,\ y = |OH| \sin \phi = r \sin \theta \sin \phi,$$
$$z = ON = r \cos \theta.$$

Also, $x^2+y^2 = |OH|^2 = r^2 \sin^2 \theta$ and $x^2+y^2+z^2 = |OP|^2 = r^2$.

Translation of axes. Just as in the plane, a given set of axes Ox, Oy, Oz can be translated through a vector $\overrightarrow{OA} = \boldsymbol{a}$ to new, parallel and similarly directed axes $A\xi$, $A\eta$, $A\zeta$. If a point P has position vector $\boldsymbol{r} = (x, y, z)$ with respect to axes Ox, Oy, Oz and position vector $\boldsymbol{\rho} = (\xi, \eta, \zeta)$ with respect to axes $A\xi$, $A\eta$, $A\zeta$ and if $\boldsymbol{a} = (x_1, y_1, z_1)$, then

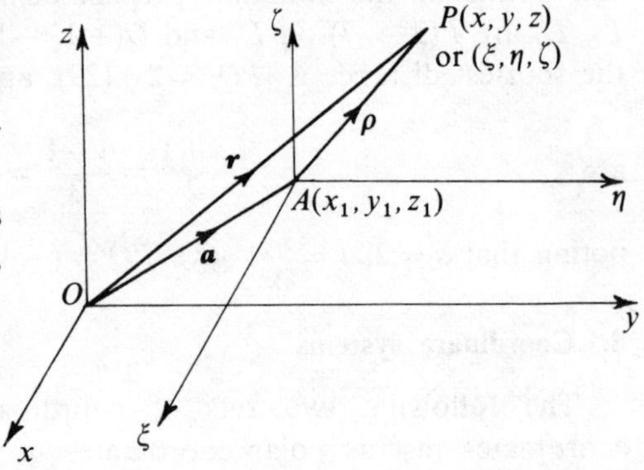

$$(\xi, \eta, \zeta) = \boldsymbol{\rho} = \overrightarrow{AP}$$
$$= \overrightarrow{OP} - \overrightarrow{OA} = \boldsymbol{r} - \boldsymbol{a}$$
$$= (x-x_1, y-y_1, z-z_1).$$

Thus $\xi = x-x_1$, $\eta = y-y_1$ and $\zeta = z-z_1$. Also $x = \xi+x_1$, $y = \eta+y_1$ and $z = \zeta+z_1$.

Rotation of axes. Suppose that rectangular axes Ox, Oy, Oz are rotated about O to positions $O\xi$, $O\eta$, $O\zeta$ and that the unit vectors $\boldsymbol{u}$, $\boldsymbol{v}$, $\boldsymbol{w}$ in directions $\overrightarrow{O\xi}$, $\overrightarrow{O\eta}$, $\overrightarrow{O\zeta}$ have components with respect to $\boldsymbol{i}$, $\boldsymbol{j}$, $\boldsymbol{k}$ given by $\boldsymbol{u} = l_1\boldsymbol{i}+m_1\boldsymbol{j}+n_1\boldsymbol{k}$, $\boldsymbol{v} = l_2\boldsymbol{i}+m_2\boldsymbol{j}+n_2\boldsymbol{k}$, and $\boldsymbol{w} = l_3\boldsymbol{i}+m_3\boldsymbol{j}+n_3\boldsymbol{k}$. Then since $\boldsymbol{u}$, $\boldsymbol{v}$, $\boldsymbol{w}$ form an orthonormal set of vectors,

$$l_i^2+m_i^2+n_i^2 = 1, \quad (i = 1, 2, 3), \tag{8.1}$$

and

$$l_i l_j + m_i m_j + n_i n_j = 0, \quad (1 \leqslant i < j \leqslant 3). \tag{8.2}$$

If a point P has coordinates (x, y, z) and (ξ, η, ζ) with respect to the two coordinate systems, then

$$\begin{aligned} x\boldsymbol{i}+y\boldsymbol{j}+z\boldsymbol{k} &= \overrightarrow{OP} = \xi\boldsymbol{u}+\eta\boldsymbol{v}+\zeta\boldsymbol{w} \\ &= \xi(l_1\boldsymbol{i}+m_1\boldsymbol{j}+n_1\boldsymbol{k})+\eta(l_2\boldsymbol{i}+m_2\boldsymbol{j}+n_2\boldsymbol{k})+\zeta(l_3\boldsymbol{i}+m_3\boldsymbol{j}+n_3\boldsymbol{k}) \\ &= (l_1\xi+l_2\eta+l_3\zeta)\boldsymbol{i}+(m_1\xi+m_2\eta+m_3\zeta)\boldsymbol{j}+(n_1\xi+n_2\eta+n_3\zeta)\boldsymbol{k}. \end{aligned}$$

Thus

$$\left\{ \begin{aligned} x &= l_1\xi+l_2\eta+l_3\zeta, \\ y &= m_1\xi+m_2\eta+m_3\zeta, \\ z &= n_1\xi+n_2\eta+n_3\zeta. \end{aligned} \right. \tag{8.3}$$

In matrix notation (8.3) can be be written as $X = TY$, where

$$X = \begin{bmatrix} x \\ y \\ z \end{bmatrix}, \quad Y = \begin{bmatrix} \xi \\ \eta \\ \zeta \end{bmatrix} \quad \text{and} \quad T = \begin{bmatrix} l_1 & l_2 & l_3 \\ m_1 & m_2 & m_3 \\ n_1 & n_2 & n_3 \end{bmatrix}.$$

Using the equations (8.1) and (8.2) it is easy to check that the matrix T is orthogonal, i.e. that $T'T = I$. Thus $T^{-1} = T'$ and the equations can be solved, in matrix form, to give $Y = T'X$.

Exercise. (i) Write out the linear equations expressing ξ, η, ζ in terms of x, y, z.

(ii) Show that $l_1^2+l_2^2+l_3^2 = 1$ and that $l_1m_1+l_2m_2+l_3m_3 = 0$ and state the four other similar equations.

9. Some simple surfaces

I. Quadrics. Any locus in 3-dimensional space which can be represented in a given coordinate system by a polynomial equation in x, y, z of second degree, i.e. by an equation of the form

$$ax^2+by^2+cz^2+2fyz+2gzx+2hxy+2ux+2vy+2wz+d = 0, \qquad (9.1)$$

where $a, b, c, d, f, g, h, u, v, w$ are real constants with a, b, c, f, g, h not all zero, is called a **quadric surface.** By translation and rotation of axes (if necessary), equation (9.1), when it represents a *non-empty locus*, can be reduced to one of the *canonical* forms listed below.

We note that in drawing such surfaces it is useful to consider their curves of intersection with the coordinate planes or parallel planes (called **plane sections**).

(1) **Ellipsoid**:

$$\frac{x^2}{a^2}+\frac{y^2}{b^2}+\frac{z^2}{c^2} = 1.$$

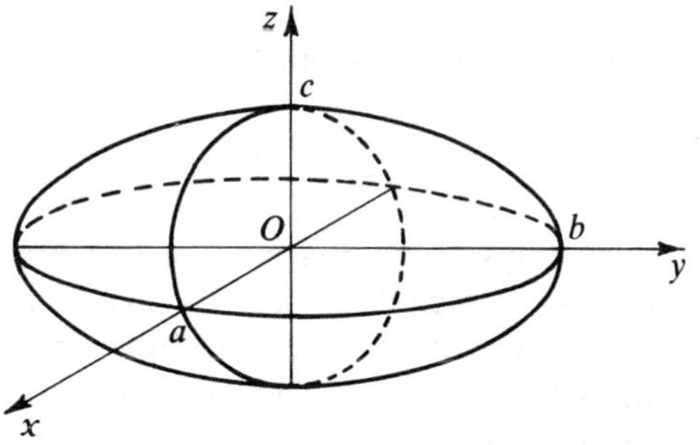

[The sphere is a particular case.]

All the non-trivial plane sections are ellipses or circles.

The x, y, z-axes are called the **principal axes** of the ellipsoid; the surface has the coordinate planes as planes of symmetry.

(2) **Hyperboloid of one sheet**:

$$\frac{x^2}{a^2}+\frac{y^2}{b^2}-\frac{z^2}{c^2}=1.$$

Sections by planes parallel to the x, y-plane are ellipses (circles when $a=b$) and sections by planes parallel to the y, z- and z, x-planes are hyperbolas.

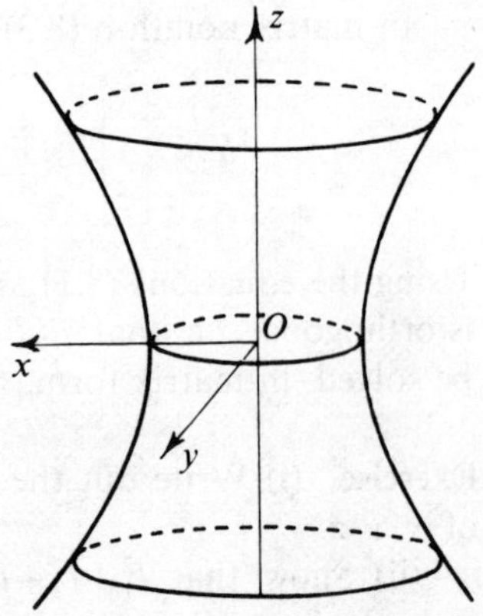

(3) **Hyperboloid of 2 sheets (or branches)**:

$$\frac{x^2}{a^2}+\frac{y^2}{b^2}-\frac{z^2}{c^2}=-1.$$

Sections by planes parallel to the x, y-plane are, when non-empty, ellipses (or circles).

Sections by planes parallel to the other coordinate planes are hyperbolas.

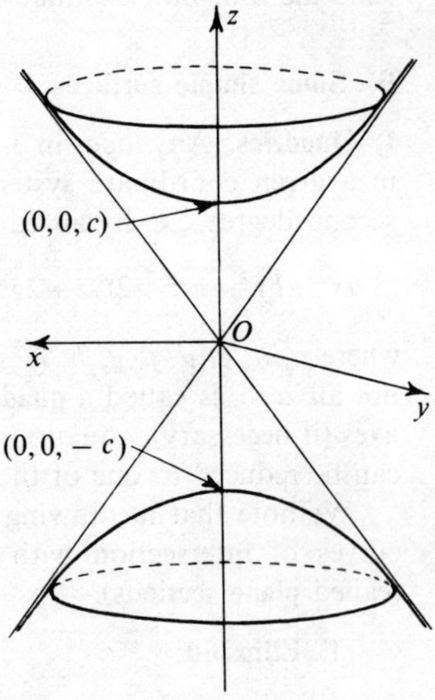

(4) **Elliptic paraboloid**:

$$\frac{x^2}{a^2}+\frac{y^2}{b^2}=2z.$$

Sections by planes $z=k(k\geqslant 0)$ are ellipses (or circles), $k=0$ giving a point circle at O. Sections by planes parallel to the other coordinate planes are parabolas.

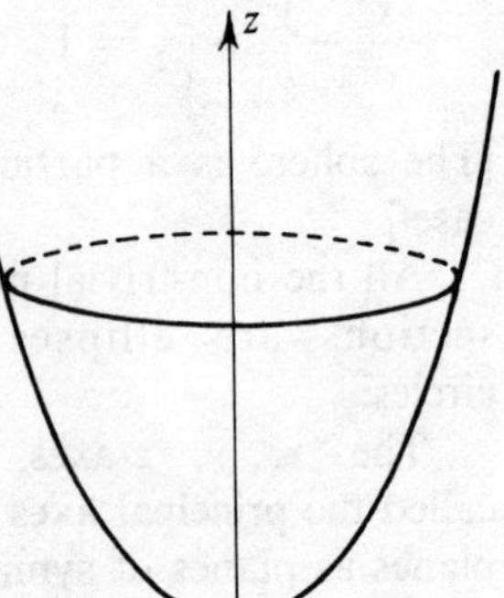

(5) **Hyperbolic paraboloid**:

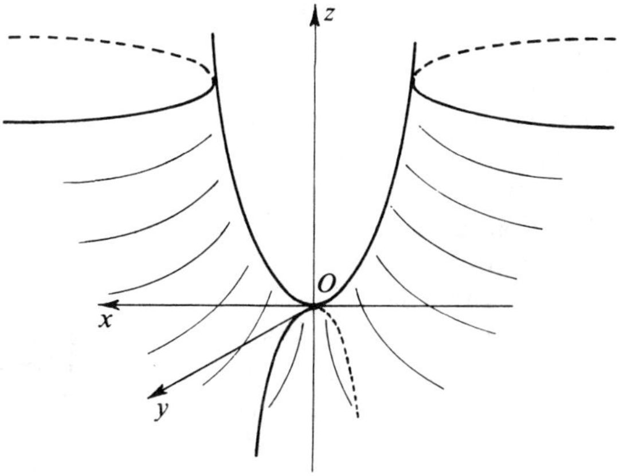

$$\frac{x^2}{a^2}-\frac{y^2}{b^2}=2z.$$

The section by the plane $z=0$ is a pair of lines, and the section by any parallel plane is a hyperbola. Sections by planes parallel to the other coordinate planes are parabolas.

O is a **saddle point** of the surface.

(6) **Cone**:

$$\frac{x^2}{a^2}+\frac{y^2}{b^2}=z^2.$$

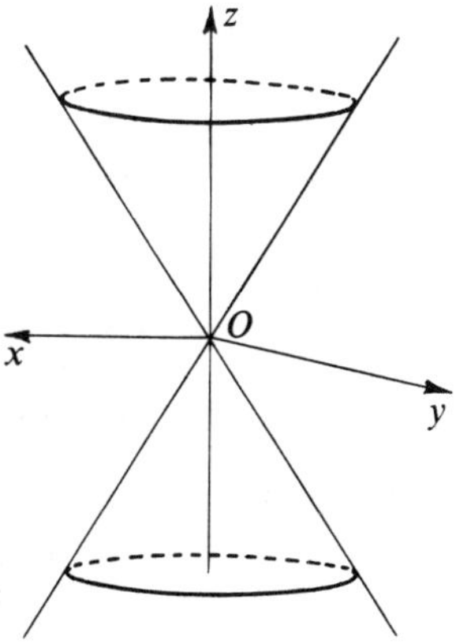

(7) **Cylinders**:

elliptic; $\quad \frac{x^2}{a^2}+\frac{y^2}{b^2}=1,$

hyperbolic; $\quad \frac{x^2}{a^2}-\frac{y^2}{b^2}=1,$

parabolic; $\quad \frac{x^2}{a^2}=2y.$

(8) **Pair of planes**:

$$\begin{cases} \text{non parallel;} & \dfrac{x^2}{a^2}=y^2, \\ \text{parallel;} & x^2=a^2. \end{cases}$$

(9) **A line**:

$$\frac{x^2}{a^2}+\frac{y^2}{b^2}=0, \quad \text{i.e. } x=y=0.$$

(10) **A point**:

$$\frac{x^2}{a^2}+\frac{y^2}{b^2}+\frac{z^2}{c^2}=0, \quad \text{i.e. } x=y=z=0.$$

II. A surface of revolution about the z-axis. For such a surface, a section by a plane parallel to the x, y-plane is, if non-empty, a circle. The surface can be generated by rotating about OZ, through one complete revolution, a plane curve, e.g. the curve of intersection of the surface with the half-plane given by $x = 0$, $y \geqslant 0$. Suppose that this curve has equations $y = f(z)$, $x = 0$ and that $A(0, f(z), z)$ is a point on the curve. The circular cross-section of the surface which passes through A has centre $L(0, 0, z)$ and a point $P(x, y, z)$ belongs to this cross-section $\Leftrightarrow |LP|^2 = |LA|^2 \Leftrightarrow x^2+y^2 = \{f(z)\}^2$.

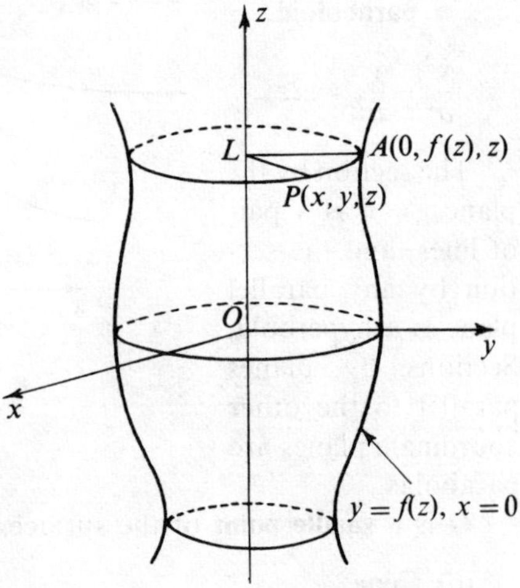

Since this argument applies to each cross-section parallel to the plane $z = 0$ it follows that the surface of revolution has equation

$$x^2+y^2 = \{f(z)\}^2. \tag{9.2}$$

Similarly, surfaces of revolution about the x-axis and the y-axis have equations of the form $y^2+z^2 = \{g(x)\}^2$ and $z^2+x^2 = \{h(y)\}^2$, respectively, for some functions g and h.

Example. *The right-circular cone, vertex O, axis Oz, semi-vertical angle α.* In this case the curve of intersection given by $x = 0$, $y \geqslant 0$ is

$$y = \begin{cases} z \tan \alpha \ (z \geqslant 0) \\ -z \tan \alpha \ (z < 0) \end{cases}, \quad x = 0.$$

Thus, in the above notation,

$$f(z) = \begin{cases} z \tan \alpha \ (z \geqslant 0) \\ -z \tan \alpha \ (z < 0), \end{cases}$$

and, from (9.2), the cone has equation

$$x^2+y^2 = z^2 \tan^2 \alpha.$$

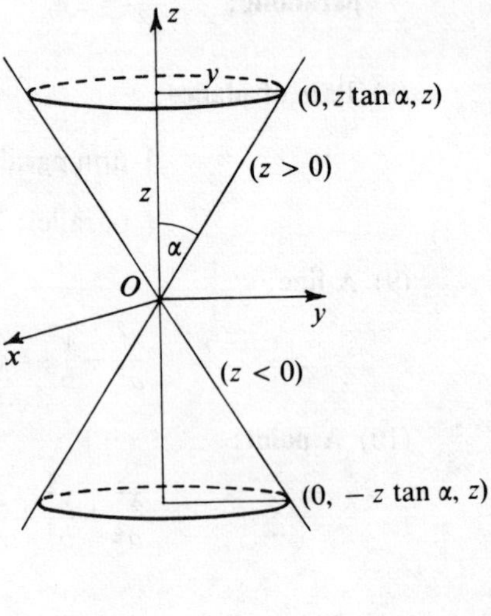

1. Find the coordinates of the point on the z-axis that is equidistant from the points $A(1, 0, 1)$ and $B(-4, 3, -1)$.
2. Find the distances from the point $A(-4, 1, 3)$ to (i) the point $B(2, -1, 0)$, (ii) the y-axis, (iii) the x, y-plane. Find the equation of the sphere with $\vec{OA}$ as a diameter.
3. Find the coordinates of the points of trisection of the line-segment joining the point $A(4, -2, 2)$ to the point $B(10, -8, 5)$. What are the reflections of the four points in the x, y-plane?
4. Show that, if A is the point $(2, 1, 0)$ and B the point $(1, 2, 4)$, then the set of points $\{P: |AP| = \sqrt{2}|BP|\}$ is a sphere, and find its centre and radius.
5. Find the equation of the sphere which passes through the circle $x^2+y^2-2x-1 = 0$, $z = 0$ and the point $A(0, 2, -1)$.
6. Find the equation of the sphere which touches the x, y-plane at the origin and passes through the point $(1, -1, 2)$.
7. Find the equation of the sphere which touches the positive x- and y-axes and passes through the points $(0, 0, 2)$ and $(0, 0, 8)$.
8. Sketch the sets

$$A = \{(x, y, z): x^2+y^2+z^2 \leqslant 2\} \quad \text{and} \quad B = \{(x, y, z): x^2+y^2 \leqslant 1\},$$

and indicate $A \cap B$.

If $C = \{(x, y, z): x^2+y^2 \leqslant 2\}$, identify $A \cap C$.

9. A has position vector $\boldsymbol{a}$, B has position vector $\boldsymbol{b}$ and C, D have position vectors $2\boldsymbol{a}+3\boldsymbol{b}$ and $\boldsymbol{a}-2\boldsymbol{b}$, respectively. Express the vectors $\vec{AC}$, $\vec{DB}$, $\vec{BC}$, $\vec{CA}$, $\vec{AC}+3\vec{DB}$ and $2\vec{DB}-5\vec{CA}$ in terms of $\boldsymbol{a}$ and $\boldsymbol{b}$.
10. Prove that for any tetrahedron the four lines obtained by joining each vertex to the centroid of the opposite triangular face are concurrent at a point which divides each of the four lines in the ratio 3:1 measured from the appropriate vertex. [The point of concurrency is called the **centroid** of the tetrahedron.]
11. If $\boldsymbol{a} = (1, 1, -2)$, $\boldsymbol{b} = (2, 1, 0)$, $\boldsymbol{c} = (-3, 5, 2)$, find the components of the vectors $\boldsymbol{a}+3\boldsymbol{b}$, $3\boldsymbol{a}-2\boldsymbol{c}$, $\boldsymbol{a}-\boldsymbol{b}+5\boldsymbol{c}$.

Find the unit vectors in the directions of $\boldsymbol{a}$, $\boldsymbol{b}$, $\boldsymbol{c}$ and $\boldsymbol{a}+3\boldsymbol{b}$.

12. Find the direction cosines of the vector $\vec{AB}$ in each of the following cases:
(a) $A(3, 2, -2)$, $B(1, 4, -3)$; (b) $A(-1, -3, 2)$, $B(2, 0, -1)$;
(c) $A(3, -1, 7)$, $B(4, -3, -1)$; (d) $A(2, 5, 3)$, $B(-3, 4, -1)$.
13. A direction makes *equal* angles of (a) $\frac{1}{3}\pi$, (b) $\frac{1}{4}\pi$ radians with the positive directions of *two* of the coordinate axes. Find in each case the angle that it makes with the positive direction of the third axis. Illustrate each situation in a diagram taking the given axes as Ox, Oy and noting all possible solutions.

If a direction makes equal angles with two of the axes, what are the smallest and largest values which this angle can take?

Which directions make equal angles with all three axes?

14. If $\vec{OA} = 2\boldsymbol{i}+\boldsymbol{j}-\boldsymbol{k}$ and $\vec{OB} = -\boldsymbol{i}+3\boldsymbol{j}-\boldsymbol{k}$, show that $\vec{AB}$ is parallel to the x, y-plane. Show in a diagram of the x, y-plane the vector in the plane which is the projection of $\vec{AB}$ on the plane.

15. Show that there are geometrical representations of the vectors $\boldsymbol{a} = \boldsymbol{i} - 3\boldsymbol{j} + 5\boldsymbol{k}$, $\boldsymbol{b} = 2\boldsymbol{i} + \boldsymbol{j} - 4\boldsymbol{k}$, $\boldsymbol{c} = 3\boldsymbol{i} - 2\boldsymbol{j} + \boldsymbol{k}$ which form a right-angled triangle.

16. Find the coordinates of the point P in the first octant, distant 28 units from the origin, for which $\overrightarrow{OP}$ has direction numbers $(2, 3, 6)$.

17. Find the vector equation, parametric equations and equations in symmetric form for each of the following lines:

(a) the line through the point $A(2, 5, 3)$ and having direction numbers $(-2, 4, -3)$;

(b) the line through the points $(-2, -1, 4)$ and $(3, 2, 2)$.

Find the point in which each of these lines meets the x, y-plane.

18. The line L passes through the point $A(1, 3, 2)$ and has direction numbers $(2, 1, -2)$. Find the coordinates of the two points on L which are at distance 3 units from A.

19. Find a value of c such that the line with parametric equations

$$x = 1 + 7t, \quad y = 2 + 3t, \quad z = 1 + ct, \quad (t \in \mathbf{R}),$$

is parallel to the line

$$x = 3 + 21k, \quad y = 2 + 9k, \quad z = 5 + 8k, \quad (k \in \mathbf{R}).$$

Show also that there is no value of c for which the lines intersect.

20. Find the coordinates of the points in which the line

$$\frac{x}{-1} = \frac{y-3}{2} = \frac{z-4}{3}$$

meets the surface $xy = z$.

21. Find the vector equation of the plane containing the two parallel lines $\boldsymbol{r} = \boldsymbol{a} + s\boldsymbol{b}\ (s \in \mathbf{R})$ and $\boldsymbol{r} = \boldsymbol{a}' + t\boldsymbol{b}\ (t \in \mathbf{R})$.

22. Find the vector equation of the line joining the points with position vectors $\boldsymbol{i} - 2\boldsymbol{j} + \boldsymbol{k}$ and $-2\boldsymbol{j} + 3\boldsymbol{k}$. Find the position vector of the point in which this line meets the plane

$$\boldsymbol{r} = p\boldsymbol{j} + q(2\boldsymbol{i} - \boldsymbol{k}), \quad p \text{ and } q \text{ parameters.}$$

23. Determine which of the following sets of points are collinear:

(a) $A(0, 5, -3)$, $B(3, -1, 12)$, $C(-2, 9, -13)$;

(b) $P(5, 1, 9)$, $Q(-1, 5, 0)$, $R(8, -1, 13)$;

(c) $L(4, 2, 3)$, $M(2, -4, 5)$, $N(6, 8, 1)$.

24. $ABCD$ is a quadrilateral in space (not necessarily in a plane), and M_1, M_2, M_3, M_4 are the midpoints of the sides AB, BC, CD, DA respectively. Prove that M_1M_3 and M_2M_4 meet and bisect each other.

25. Prove that for any tetrahedron the three lines joining the midpoints of opposite edges bisect each other.

26. If $\boldsymbol{u} = \boldsymbol{i} + 2\boldsymbol{j}$, $\boldsymbol{v} = 2\boldsymbol{i} - \boldsymbol{j} + 3\boldsymbol{k}$ and $\boldsymbol{w} = -\boldsymbol{i} + 13\boldsymbol{j} - 9\boldsymbol{k}$, show that $\boldsymbol{w}$ is coplanar with $\boldsymbol{u}$ and $\boldsymbol{v}$.

27. Show that the vectors $\boldsymbol{u} = \boldsymbol{i} + \boldsymbol{j}$, $\boldsymbol{v} = \boldsymbol{i} - \boldsymbol{j}$, $\boldsymbol{w} = 2\boldsymbol{i} + \boldsymbol{j} + \boldsymbol{k}$ form a basis for 3-dimensional euclidean space.

If $x\boldsymbol{i} + y\boldsymbol{j} + z\boldsymbol{k} = \xi\boldsymbol{u} + \eta\boldsymbol{v} + \zeta\boldsymbol{w}$, express x, y, z in terms of ξ, η, ζ and ξ, η, ζ in terms of x, y, z.

28. Show that the vectors $\boldsymbol{u} = \boldsymbol{i} + 3\boldsymbol{j} - 2\boldsymbol{k}$, $\boldsymbol{v} = 2\boldsymbol{i} - \boldsymbol{j} + \boldsymbol{k}$, $\boldsymbol{w} = -2\boldsymbol{i} + \boldsymbol{j} - 3\boldsymbol{k}$ form a basis for 3-dimensional euclidean space, and find the components of the vector $\boldsymbol{a} = 3\boldsymbol{i} + 2\boldsymbol{j} + 5\boldsymbol{k}$ with respect to this basis.

29. Show that the vectors $\boldsymbol{u} = \boldsymbol{i}+\boldsymbol{j}+\boldsymbol{k}$, $\boldsymbol{v} = \boldsymbol{i}-\boldsymbol{j}+\boldsymbol{k}$, $\boldsymbol{w} = 2\boldsymbol{i}-\boldsymbol{k}$ form a basis for 3-dimensional euclidean space, and find the components of the vector $5\boldsymbol{i}+3\boldsymbol{j}+2\boldsymbol{k}$ with respect to this basis.

If $a\boldsymbol{u}+b\boldsymbol{v}+c\boldsymbol{w} = x\boldsymbol{i}+y\boldsymbol{j}+z\boldsymbol{k}$, show that

$$a+b+c = 1 \Leftrightarrow 2x+z = 3.$$

30. A, B, C are distinct points with position vectors $\boldsymbol{a}$, $\boldsymbol{b}$, $\boldsymbol{c}$, respectively. Prove that A, B, C are collinear if and only if there exist scalars λ, μ, ν, not all zero, such that

$$\lambda\boldsymbol{a}+\mu\boldsymbol{b}+\nu\boldsymbol{c} = \boldsymbol{0} \quad \text{and} \quad \lambda+\mu+\nu = 0.$$

31. Show that the vector $\boldsymbol{a} = -\boldsymbol{i}-4\boldsymbol{j}+7\boldsymbol{k}$ is coplanar with the vectors $\boldsymbol{u} = 2\boldsymbol{i}+3\boldsymbol{j}-\boldsymbol{k}$ and $\boldsymbol{v} = 4\boldsymbol{i}+\boldsymbol{j}+11\boldsymbol{k}$. Find a vector which is coplanar with these three vectors and is perpendicular to $\boldsymbol{a}$.

32. (i) Show that the triangle with vertices $P(1, 1, 1)$, $Q(-1, -2, 0)$, $R(0, -6, 1)$ is obtuse-angled at Q.
(ii) Find k so that lines with direction numbers $(1, 2, k)$ and $(-4, 1, -2)$ are perpendicular.

33. Show that (i) $|\boldsymbol{a}.\boldsymbol{b}| \leqslant |\boldsymbol{a}||\boldsymbol{b}|$, (ii) $(\boldsymbol{a}\times\boldsymbol{b})^2 = \boldsymbol{a}^2\boldsymbol{b}^2-(\boldsymbol{a}.\boldsymbol{b})^2$. When does equality hold in (i)?

34. If $\boldsymbol{a} = 2\boldsymbol{i}+2\boldsymbol{j}-\boldsymbol{k}$, $\boldsymbol{b} = \boldsymbol{i}-\boldsymbol{j}+3\boldsymbol{k}$, $\boldsymbol{c} = 2\boldsymbol{i}-3\boldsymbol{j}+\boldsymbol{k}$, find (i) $\boldsymbol{b}.\boldsymbol{c}$, (ii) the scalar projection of $\boldsymbol{c}$ on $\boldsymbol{a}$, (iii) the cosine of the angle between $\boldsymbol{a}$ and $\boldsymbol{c}$, (iv) $\boldsymbol{b}\times\boldsymbol{c}$, (v) $[\boldsymbol{a}, \boldsymbol{b}, \boldsymbol{c}]$, (vi) $\boldsymbol{a}\times(\boldsymbol{b}\times\boldsymbol{c})$.

35. Simplify $(\boldsymbol{a}+\boldsymbol{b}).(\boldsymbol{a}-\boldsymbol{b})$ and $(\boldsymbol{a}+\boldsymbol{b})\times(\boldsymbol{a}-\boldsymbol{b})$; show that $\boldsymbol{a}+\boldsymbol{b}$ and $\boldsymbol{a}-\boldsymbol{b}$ are perpendicular if and only if $|\boldsymbol{a}| = |\boldsymbol{b}|$.

36. Find the unit vector in the direction of the vector $2\boldsymbol{m}-\boldsymbol{n}$, where $\boldsymbol{m}$, $\boldsymbol{n}$ are unit vectors at an angle $\frac{1}{4}\pi$ to one another.

37. Find the area of a parallelogram with diagonals determined by the vectors $\boldsymbol{a} = 2\boldsymbol{i}+3\boldsymbol{j}-\boldsymbol{k}$ and $\boldsymbol{b} = \boldsymbol{j}+3\boldsymbol{k}$.

38. A plane passes through the points A, B, C with position vectors $\boldsymbol{a}$, $\boldsymbol{b}$, $\boldsymbol{c}$. Show that $\boldsymbol{a}\times\boldsymbol{b}+\boldsymbol{b}\times\boldsymbol{c}+\boldsymbol{c}\times\boldsymbol{a}$ is a normal vector to the plane.

39. Show that the vectors $|\boldsymbol{b}|\boldsymbol{a}\pm|\boldsymbol{a}|\boldsymbol{b}$ give directions of the bisectors of the angles between the non-zero, non-parallel vectors $\boldsymbol{a}$, $\boldsymbol{b}$.

40. Find the cosine of the acute angle between the diagonal of a cube and (a) one of its edges, (b) a diagonal of one of its faces.

[**Note.** The cube may be taken as the coordinate cube of the point with coordinates $(1, 1, 1)$.]

41. In tetrahedron $ABCD$, edge AB is perpendicular to edge CD and edge AC is perpendicular to edge BD. Prove that

$$(\boldsymbol{a}.\boldsymbol{c})+(\boldsymbol{b}.\boldsymbol{d}) = (\boldsymbol{a}.\boldsymbol{d})+(\boldsymbol{b}.\boldsymbol{c}) = (\boldsymbol{a}.\boldsymbol{b})+(\boldsymbol{c}.\boldsymbol{d}),$$

and deduce that edge AD is perpendicular to edge BC.

42. In triangle OAB, $\overrightarrow{OA} = \boldsymbol{a}$, $\overrightarrow{OB} = \boldsymbol{b}$ and the perpendicular bisectors of sides OA and OB meet at C. If $\overrightarrow{OC} = \boldsymbol{c}$, show that $\boldsymbol{c}.\boldsymbol{a} = \frac{1}{2}\boldsymbol{a}^2$, $\boldsymbol{c}.\boldsymbol{b} = \frac{1}{2}\boldsymbol{b}^2$, and deduce by vector methods that the join of C to the midpoint of side AB is perpendicular to AB.

43. Prove that $[\boldsymbol{u}_1+\boldsymbol{u}_2, \boldsymbol{v}, \boldsymbol{w}] = [\boldsymbol{u}_1, \boldsymbol{v}, \boldsymbol{w}]+[\boldsymbol{u}_2, \boldsymbol{v}, \boldsymbol{w}]$, and hence show that $[\boldsymbol{a}+\boldsymbol{b}, \boldsymbol{b}+\boldsymbol{c}, \boldsymbol{c}+\boldsymbol{a}] = 2[\boldsymbol{a}, \boldsymbol{b}, \boldsymbol{c}]$.

44. Show that (i) if $\boldsymbol{a}+\boldsymbol{b}+\boldsymbol{c}=\boldsymbol{0}$, then $\boldsymbol{a}\times\boldsymbol{b}=\boldsymbol{b}\times\boldsymbol{c}=\boldsymbol{c}\times\boldsymbol{a}$; (ii) $\boldsymbol{a}\times(\boldsymbol{b}\times\boldsymbol{c})+\boldsymbol{b}\times(\boldsymbol{c}\times\boldsymbol{a})+\boldsymbol{c}\times(\boldsymbol{a}\times\boldsymbol{b})=\boldsymbol{0}$; (iii) $(\boldsymbol{a}\times\boldsymbol{b})\times(\boldsymbol{a}\times\boldsymbol{c})=[\boldsymbol{a},\boldsymbol{b},\boldsymbol{c}]\boldsymbol{a}$; (iv $(\boldsymbol{a}\times\boldsymbol{b})\times(\boldsymbol{c}\times\boldsymbol{d})=[\boldsymbol{a},\boldsymbol{b},\boldsymbol{d}]\boldsymbol{c}-[\boldsymbol{a},\boldsymbol{b},\boldsymbol{c}]\boldsymbol{d}$; (v) $[\boldsymbol{a}\times\boldsymbol{b},\boldsymbol{b}\times\boldsymbol{c},\boldsymbol{c}\times\boldsymbol{a}]=[\boldsymbol{a},\boldsymbol{b},\boldsymbol{c}]^2$.

45. $\boldsymbol{a}$, $\boldsymbol{b}$, $\boldsymbol{c}$ are non-coplanar vectors and $\boldsymbol{d}$ is any vector. By using the identity $(\boldsymbol{a}\times\boldsymbol{b})\times(\boldsymbol{c}\times\boldsymbol{d})=-(\boldsymbol{c}\times\boldsymbol{d})\times(\boldsymbol{a}\times\boldsymbol{b})$, show that

$$\boldsymbol{d}=\frac{1}{[\boldsymbol{a},\boldsymbol{b},\boldsymbol{c}]}\{[\boldsymbol{d},\boldsymbol{b},\boldsymbol{c}]\boldsymbol{a}+[\boldsymbol{d},\boldsymbol{c},\boldsymbol{a}]\boldsymbol{b}+[\boldsymbol{d},\boldsymbol{a},\boldsymbol{b}]\boldsymbol{c}\}.$$

46. Express $\{\boldsymbol{d}\times(\boldsymbol{c}\times\boldsymbol{a})\}\times(\boldsymbol{a}\times\boldsymbol{b})$ in the form $\lambda\boldsymbol{a}+\mu\boldsymbol{b}$ with λ, μ scalars.

47. If $\boldsymbol{x}$ is a vector such that

$$\boldsymbol{x}.\boldsymbol{a}=k \quad\text{and}\quad \boldsymbol{x}\times\boldsymbol{b}=\boldsymbol{c}, \tag{1}$$

where k is a given scalar and $\boldsymbol{a}$, $\boldsymbol{b}$, $\boldsymbol{c}$ are given vectors such that $\boldsymbol{a}.\boldsymbol{b}\neq 0$ and $\boldsymbol{b}.\boldsymbol{c}=0$, show, by considering $\boldsymbol{a}\times(\boldsymbol{x}\times\boldsymbol{b})$, that $\boldsymbol{x}=(1/\boldsymbol{a}.\boldsymbol{b})\{k\boldsymbol{b}+\boldsymbol{a}\times\boldsymbol{c}\}$. Hence show that this vector is the unique solution of the pair of equations (1). [**Note.** $\boldsymbol{x}\times\boldsymbol{b}=\boldsymbol{c}\Rightarrow\boldsymbol{b}.\boldsymbol{x}\times\boldsymbol{b}=\boldsymbol{b}.\boldsymbol{c}\Rightarrow 0=\boldsymbol{b}.\boldsymbol{c}$.]

48. Show that the vector equation $\boldsymbol{x}+(\boldsymbol{x}\times\boldsymbol{u})=\boldsymbol{v}$, where $\boldsymbol{u}$ and $\boldsymbol{v}$ are given vectors, has a unique solution for $\boldsymbol{x}$. [*Hint.* Take the vector product and scalar product of $\boldsymbol{u}$ with both sides.]

49. Find an equation for each of the following planes:

(i) the plane perpendicular to the line

$$\frac{x-3}{2}=\frac{y+2}{1}=\frac{z-4}{6}$$

and through the point $P(3,-2,4)$;

(ii) the plane perpendicular to the line determined by the points $A(0,4,0)$ and $B(-6,-5,-4)$, and through $C(1,2,3)$;

(iii) the plane parallel to the plane $x-2y+z=5$ and through the point $A(1,-1,0)$;

(iv) the plane perpendicular to the line

$$\begin{cases} x-2y+z=4,\\ 2x+y-z=5,\end{cases}$$

and through the point $A(4,5,-3)$;

(v) the plane through the points $A(0,-1,2)$, $B(1,2,-3)$, $C(-1,2,3)$;

(vi) the plane through the points $P(5,2,1)$ and $Q(2,1,-1)$ and parallel to the z-axis.

50. (i) Find the equation of the sphere with centre $C(1,2,-1)$ which touches the plane $y-4z+11=0$.

(ii) Find the equations of the tangent planes to the sphere $x^2+y^2+z^2=1$ which are parallel to the plane $2x-y+2z+6=0$.

51. Find the coordinates of the foot of the perpendicular from the point $A(1,3,2)$ to the plane $2x+2y-z+3=0$.

52. Find equations in symmetric form and parametric equations for the line of intersection of the planes $6x+y-z+2=0$ and $2x-y+3z-14=0$.

53. Find the equation of the plane π_1 which projects the line L:

$$\frac{x-2}{2}=\frac{y+1}{3}=\frac{z+3}{-1}$$

on to the plane $\pi: 2x+y+5z+16=0$.

54. Find an equation for the plane which passes through the line L:
$$\frac{x-1}{-1}=\frac{y}{1}=\frac{z+1}{1}$$
and is parallel to the direction $(1, -17, -7)$.

55. Show that the lines
$$\frac{x+3}{4}=\frac{y-4}{-7}=\frac{z+1}{3} \quad \text{and} \quad \frac{x-5}{2}=\frac{y-3}{3}=\frac{z+6}{-4}$$
are coplanar, and find the equation of the plane containing them.

56. Show that the points $A(0, -1, 0)$, $B(2, 1, -1)$, $C(1, 1, 1)$, $D(3, 3, 0)$ are coplanar, finding the equation of the plane containing them.

57. Find the foot of the perpendicular from the point $A(1, 0, -1)$ to the line:
$$\frac{x-3}{1}=\frac{y-4}{3}=\frac{z-2}{-1},$$
and hence find the perpendicular distance from A to L.

58. Find the equation of the plane through the line of intersection of the planes $7x+z-6=0$, $17x+y-18=0$ and the point $A(1, 2, 2)$. [*Hint.* Consider the equation
$$7x+z-6+k(17x+y-18)=0 \quad \text{for} \quad k\in\mathbf{R},$$
and see Example 1, Section 4, Part 1.]

59. Show that the line $\begin{cases} x-3y+6=0 \\ x-2z-4=0 \end{cases}$ lies in the plane $x-9y+4z+26=0$.

60. L is the line $\dfrac{x-1}{1}=\dfrac{y+2}{1}=\dfrac{z-1}{-1}$. Show that, for every real number k, the equation $x-y-3+k(y+z+1)=0$ represents a plane containing L. [Is every plane containing L representable in this way?] Hence find the equations of the two planes through L that make an angle $\frac{1}{3}\pi$ with the plane $2x-y+z=0$.

61. Describe the subsets $\{(x, y, z): ax+by+cz+d>0\}$ and $\{(x, y, z): ax+by+cz+d<0\}$, where a, b, c, d are constants with a, b, c not all zero.

62. Find the sine of the acute angle which the line $L: \dfrac{x-3}{2}=\dfrac{y+2}{-1}=\dfrac{z-3}{3}$ makes with the plane $\pi: 3x+2y-z=5$.

63. Find the length of and equations in symmetric form for the shortest distance between the lines
$$\frac{x-3}{0}=\frac{y}{-2}=\frac{z-5}{1} \quad \text{and} \quad \frac{x+2}{3}=\frac{y+1}{2}=\frac{z+1}{-2}$$
and the coordinates of the points at which it meets the lines.

64. (i) Show that the planes $x-y-3z=3$, $x+2y-4z=7$ and $2x-y=1$ meet at one point.
(ii) Determine the nature of the set of points common to the three planes $x+y+z=6$, $5x+5y+5z=1$ and $x-y=10$.

65. Find the vertices of the tetrahedron whose faces lie in the planes $x-y=0$, $y-z=0$, $x+y=1$ and $z=0$, and sketch the tetrahedron.

66. Find the equation of the cylinder with generators parallel to the z-axis which passes through the circle in which the plane $y+z=2$ cuts the sphere $x^2+y^2+z^2=6$. Draw the section of the cylinder by the plane $z=0$.

67. Find the equations in terms of spherical polar coordinates for each of the following surfaces (i) $x^2+y^2+z^2 = 1$, (ii) $x^2+y^2 = 1$, (iii) $x^2+y^2 = z^2$, (iv) $x-y = 0$, (v) $z = 1$.

68. P' is the projection of the point P on the line through the point A (with position vector $\boldsymbol{a}$) for which $\boldsymbol{v}$ is a direction vector. Prove that $|PP'| = |(\boldsymbol{r}_P-\boldsymbol{a})\times\boldsymbol{v}|/|\boldsymbol{v}|$. Deduce that the right-circular cylinder of radius 1 whose axis is the line $x = y = z$ has equation $(y-z)^2+(z-x)^2+(x-y)^2 = 3$.

69. The vectors $\boldsymbol{u} = (\frac{2}{3}, \frac{2}{3}, -\frac{1}{3})$, $\boldsymbol{v} = (\frac{2}{3}, -\frac{1}{3}, x)$, $\boldsymbol{w} = (a, b, c)$ form a right-handed orthonormal set of vectors. Determine the components x, a, b, c.

70. If the axes Ox, Oy, Oz are rotated to the positions determined respectively by the unit vectors $\boldsymbol{u}$, $\boldsymbol{v}$, $\boldsymbol{w}$ in example **69**, write down the equations, corresponding to (8.3), for the resulting change of coordinates. Find the equation in terms of the new coordinates of the quadric surface given by the equation

$$7x^2+y^2+z^2+8xy+8xz-16yz = 9,$$

and hence determine the nature of the quadric.

Answers

Answers

Part 1.

Exercise, p. 7. $(\frac{1}{3}(x_A+x_B+x_C), \frac{1}{3}(y_A+y_B+y_C))$.

Exercise, p. 10. (a) $\{(x, y): x<0, y>0\}$, $\{(x, y): x<0, y<0\}$, $\{(x, y): x>0, y<0\}$; (b) $\{(x, y): y=0, x<0\}$; (c) $\{(x, y): x=0, y>0\}$; (d) $\{(1-t)(1, 0)+t(3, 0): 0 \leqslant t \leqslant 1\}$.

Exercise, p. 38. $\dfrac{x}{a}\sec\theta-\dfrac{y}{b}\tan\theta=1$.

Exercise 1.

2. $x^2+y^2-2x-6y=0$. **3.** $x^2+y^2=20$. **4.** $x^2+y^2-2x+2y-23=0$.
5. ± 2. **6.** (i) $2x-13y+10=0$, (ii) $27x+27y-25=0$.
8. $x=-2$, $3x+4y-10=0$. **10.** $(2, -1)$. **11.** $(0, 7/3)$.
13. Region between lines $x-y=0$ and $x-2y=0$, second region is $\{(x, y): (x-y)(x-2y)<0, 2x+y+4<0\} \cup \{(x, y): (x-y)(x-2y)>0, 2x+y+4>0\}$.
14. 30 (20 nuclear-powered and 10 coal-fired). **15.** max. value is 24, given by $x=4$, $y=3$; min. value is 17 given by $x=3$, $y=2$.
16. $x=24$, $y=8$; 240 additional personnel. **17.** max. value 15 at point $(1, 7)$; min. value -5 at point $(5, -5)$. **18.** Mine 1 for 8 days, mine 2 for 32 days; surplus of high-grade coal. **19.** 17 of type A, 6 of type B.
20. (i) $r=1$, (ii) $r=2a\cos\theta$, (iii) $r=2b\sin\theta$, (iv) $r=2/\cos\theta$, $-\frac{1}{2}\pi<\theta<\frac{1}{2}\pi$.
21. $Q(\sqrt{2}, \frac{1}{4}\pi)$, $r=\sqrt{3}$. **22.** $\xi^2=-4a\eta$, $\xi^2/b^2+\eta^2/a^2=1$; $(y'+2)^2=4a(x'+1)$, $(x'+1)^2/a^2+(y'+2)^2/b^2=1$. **24.** S is reflection in the x-axis, T reflection in $y=x$ and U is the rotation about O through angle $\frac{1}{4}\pi$; the matrices are

$$\begin{bmatrix} 0 & 1 \\ -1 & 0 \end{bmatrix}, \frac{1}{\sqrt{2}}\begin{bmatrix} 1 & -1 \\ -1 & -1 \end{bmatrix}, \frac{1}{\sqrt{2}}\begin{bmatrix} 1 & 1 \\ 1 & -1 \end{bmatrix}, \begin{bmatrix} 0 & -1 \\ 1 & 0 \end{bmatrix}, \frac{1}{\sqrt{2}}\begin{bmatrix} 1 & 1 \\ 1 & -1 \end{bmatrix}, \frac{1}{\sqrt{2}}\begin{bmatrix} -1 & 1 \\ 1 & 1 \end{bmatrix}$$

and the transformations are, respectively, rotation through $-\frac{1}{2}\pi$, reflection in line making angle $-\frac{1}{8}\pi$ with Ox, reflection in line making angle $\frac{1}{8}\pi$ with Ox, rotation through $\frac{1}{2}\pi$, reflection in line making angle $\frac{1}{8}\pi$ with Ox, reflection in line making angle $\frac{3}{8}\pi$ with Ox.
25. The result is not true for reflections in distinct lines.
26. $E: x'=2x-1$, $y'=2y$; $R_\circ E: x'=-\frac{1}{2}(2x-1)+y\sqrt{3}$, $y'=\frac{1}{2}\sqrt{3}(2x-1)+y$; fixed point $(\frac{1}{2}, 1/(2\sqrt{3}))$. **27.** $x'=11-y$, $y'=6-x$.
29. $x'=ax$, $y'=ay$; $a/a_1=b/b_1$ (taking a, b, a_1, b_1 positive).
30. (i) $z'=z-h$, $z'=z(\cos\alpha-i\sin\alpha)$, $z'=\bar{z}$, $z'=z/a$ $(a \neq 0)$.
31. $x^2+y^2=1$. **32.** (i) vertex $(1, -1)$, focus $(3, -1)$, axis $y+1=0$, directrix $x=-1$; (ii) vertex $(-3/2, 2)$, focus $(-2, 2)$, axis $y-2=0$, directrix $x=-1$.
34. Common focus is the origin $(0, 0)$.

36. Equation is $\dfrac{\xi^2}{16}+\dfrac{\eta^2}{12} = 1$, where $\xi = x+4, \eta = y-1$; $e = \frac{1}{2}$; foci are $(-6, 1)$ and $(-2, 1)$. **37.** (i) $e = \frac{1}{4}$, $(x-3)^2/64 + y^2/60 = 1$; (ii) $e = 3/5$, $(x+2)^2/25 + (y-2)^2/16 = 1$; (iii) $e = \frac{}{4}$, $(x+2)^2/64 + (y-4)^2/28 = 1$.
41. $|AP|+|CP|$ = radius of fixed circle. **42.** $\frac{1}{4}\xi^2+\eta^2 = 1$; foci $(\sqrt{3}/\sqrt{2}, \sqrt{3}/\sqrt{2})$, and $(-\sqrt{3}/\sqrt{2}, -\sqrt{3}/\sqrt{2})$. **43.** Equation is $\xi^2/5-\eta^2/20 = 1$, where $\xi = x-3$, $\eta = y+2$; foci $(-2, -2)$, $(8, -2)$; asymptotes $2x+y-4 = 0$, $2x-y-8 = 0$.
44. $C(-1,0)$; $(x+1)^2/36-y^2/45 = 1$; asymptotes $2y \pm (x+1)\sqrt{5} = 0$.
45. Transverse axis $y = x$, conjugate axis $y = -x$; asymptotes are the coordinate axes $y = 0$ and $x = 0$. **47.** $-\xi^2/2+\eta^2/3 = 1$; transverse axis $x+2y = 0$ (i.e. $\xi = 0$), conjugate axis $2x-y = 0$ (i.e. $\eta = 0$); this hyperbola is the conjugate of that in problem **23.**

Part 2.

Exercise, p. 78. $\dfrac{x+1}{1} = \dfrac{y+2}{2} = \dfrac{z}{1}$.

Exercise, p. 83. $\xi = l_1x+m_1y+n_1z$, $\eta = l_2x+m_2y+n_2z$, $\zeta = l_3x+m_3y+n_3z$; $m_1^2+m_2^2+m_3^2 = 1$, $n_1^2+n_2^2+n_3^2 = 1$, $l_1n_1+l_2n_2+l_3n_3 = 0$, $m_1n_1+m_2n_2+m_3n_3 = 0$.

Exercise 2.

1. $(0,0,-6)$. **2.** (i) 7, (ii) 5, (iii) 3; $x^2+y^2+z^2+4x-y-3z = 0$.
3. $(6, -4, 3)$, $(8, -6, 4)$; $(4, -2, -2)$, $(6, -4, -3)$, $(8, -6, -4)$, $(10, -8, -5)$.
4. Centre $(0, 3, 8)$, radius 6. **5.** $x^2+y^2+z^2-2x+4z-1 = 0$.
6. $x^2+y^2+z^2-3z = 0$. **7.** $x^2+y^2+z^2-8x-8y-10z+16 = 0$.
8. $A \cap C = A$. **9.** $\vec{AC} = \boldsymbol{a}+3\boldsymbol{b}$, $\vec{DB} = -\boldsymbol{a}+3\boldsymbol{b}$, $\vec{BC} = 2\boldsymbol{a}+2\boldsymbol{b}$, $\vec{CA} = -\boldsymbol{a}-3\boldsymbol{b}$, $\vec{AC}+3\vec{DB} = -2\boldsymbol{a}+12\boldsymbol{b}$, $2\vec{DB}-5\vec{CA} = 3\boldsymbol{a}+21\boldsymbol{b}$.
11. $(7, 4, -2)$, $(9, -7, -10)$, $(-16, 25, 8)$; $(1/\sqrt{6})(1, 1, -2)$, $(1/\sqrt{5})(2, 1, 0)$, $(1/\sqrt{(38)})(-3, 5, 2)$, $(1/\sqrt{(69)})(7, 4, -2)$. **12.** (a) $(-\frac{2}{3}, \frac{2}{3}, -\frac{1}{3})$, (b) $(1/\sqrt{3})(1, 1, -1)$, (c) $(1/\sqrt{(69)})(1, -2, -8)$, (d) $(1/\sqrt{(42)})(-5, -1, -4)$.
13. (a) $\frac{1}{4}\pi$ or $\frac{3}{4}\pi$, (b) $\frac{1}{2}\pi$; 0, π; directions $(1, 1, 1)$ and $(-1, -1, -1)$.
14. $\vec{AB} = -3\boldsymbol{i}+2\boldsymbol{j} = \vec{OC}$, where O is the origin and C the point $(-3, 2, 0)$.
15. Check that $\boldsymbol{a}+\boldsymbol{b} = \boldsymbol{c}$ and $|\boldsymbol{b}|^2+|\boldsymbol{c}|^2 = 35 = |\boldsymbol{a}|^2$.
16. $P(8, 12, 24)$. **17.** (a) $\boldsymbol{r} = (2, 5, 3)+t(-2, 4, -3)$; $x = 2-2t$, $y = 5+4t$, $z = 3-3t$; $\dfrac{x-2}{-2} = \dfrac{y-5}{4} = \dfrac{z-3}{-3}$; meets x, y-plane at point $(0, 9, 0)$;
(b) $\boldsymbol{r} = (-2, -1, 4)+t(5, 3, -2)$; $x = -2+5t$, $y = -1+3t$, $z = 4-2t$; $\dfrac{x+2}{5} = \dfrac{y+1}{3} = \dfrac{z-4}{-2}$; meets x, y-plane at point $(8, 5, 0)$.
18. $(3, 4, 0)$, $(-1, 2, 4)$. **19.** $c = \frac{8}{3}$. **20.** $(1, 1, 1)$, $(2, -1, -2)$.
21. $\boldsymbol{r} = (1-s)\boldsymbol{a}+s\boldsymbol{a}'+t\boldsymbol{b}$. **22.** $\boldsymbol{r} = (1+t)\boldsymbol{i}-2\boldsymbol{j}+(1-2t)\boldsymbol{k}$, $(t \in \mathbf{R})$; $2\boldsymbol{i}-2\boldsymbol{j}-\boldsymbol{k}$. **23.** (a) and (c). **26.** $\boldsymbol{w} = 5\boldsymbol{u}-3\boldsymbol{v}$.
27. $x = \xi+\eta+2\zeta$, $y = \xi-\eta+\zeta$, $z = \zeta$; $2\xi = x+y-3z$, $2\eta = x-y-z$, $\zeta = z$.
28. $(1, -2, -3)$. **29.** $(3, 0, 1)$. **31.** $\boldsymbol{a} = (-\frac{3}{2})\boldsymbol{u}+\frac{1}{2}\boldsymbol{v}$; $23\boldsymbol{u}+7\boldsymbol{v}$.
32. (i) $\cos \angle PQR = -3/2\sqrt{7}$; (ii) $k = -1$. **33.** Equality holds in (i) if either at least one of $\boldsymbol{a}$, $\boldsymbol{b}$ is $\boldsymbol{0}$ or the angle between $\boldsymbol{a}$ and $\boldsymbol{b}$ is 0 or π.

34. (i) 8, (ii) -1, (iii) $-1/\sqrt{(14)}$, (iv) $8\boldsymbol{i}+5\boldsymbol{j}-\boldsymbol{k}$, (v) 27, (vi) $3\boldsymbol{i}-6\boldsymbol{j}-6\boldsymbol{k}$.
35. $(\boldsymbol{a}+\boldsymbol{b}).(\boldsymbol{a}-\boldsymbol{b}) = \boldsymbol{a}^2-\boldsymbol{b}^2$, $(\boldsymbol{a}+\boldsymbol{b})\times(\boldsymbol{a}-\boldsymbol{b}) = -2\boldsymbol{a}\times\boldsymbol{b}$.
36. $\big(1/(5-4\sqrt{2})\big)(2\boldsymbol{m}-\boldsymbol{n})$. **37.** Area is $\frac{1}{2}|\boldsymbol{a}\times\boldsymbol{b}| = \sqrt{(35)}$.

38. Consider $\overrightarrow{AB}\times\overrightarrow{AC}$. **40.** (a) $1/\sqrt{3}$, (b) $\sqrt{2}/\sqrt{3}$.
46. $\lambda = (\boldsymbol{a}\times\boldsymbol{c}).(\boldsymbol{d}\times\boldsymbol{b}) = (\boldsymbol{a}.\boldsymbol{d})(\boldsymbol{b}.\boldsymbol{c})-(\boldsymbol{a}.\boldsymbol{b})(\boldsymbol{c}.\boldsymbol{d})$, $\mu = (\boldsymbol{a}\times\boldsymbol{d}).(\boldsymbol{a}\times\boldsymbol{c})$
$= \boldsymbol{a}^2(\boldsymbol{c}.\boldsymbol{d})-(\boldsymbol{a}.\boldsymbol{c})(\boldsymbol{a}.\boldsymbol{d})$. **48.** $(1+\boldsymbol{u}^2)\boldsymbol{x} = (\boldsymbol{u}.\boldsymbol{v})\boldsymbol{u}+\boldsymbol{v}+\boldsymbol{u}\times\boldsymbol{v}$.
49. (i) $2x+y+6z = 28$, (ii) $6x+9y+4z = 36$, (iii) $x-2y+z = 3$,
(iv) $x+3y+5z = 4$, (v) $9x+2y+3z = 4$, (vi) $x-3y = -1$.
50. (i) $(x-1)^2+(y-2)^2+(z+1)^2 = 17$, (ii) $2x-y+2z\pm 3 = 0$.
51. $(-1, 1, 3)$. **52.** $\dfrac{x}{1} = \dfrac{y-4}{-10} = \dfrac{z-6}{-4}$; $x = t, y = 4-10t, z = 6-4t$.
53. $4x-3y-z = 14$. **54.** $5x-3y+8z = -3$. **55.** $19x+22y+26z = 5$.
56. $4x-3y+2z = 3$. **57.** (2, 1, 3), perpendicular distance is $3\sqrt{2}$.
58. $44x+3y-z-48 = 0$. **60.** Every plane except $x-y-3 = 0$;
$x+y+2z-1 = 0$, $x-2y-z-4 = 0$.
61. The open half-spaces on each side of the plane $ax+by+cz+d = 0$.
62. $\frac{1}{14}$. **63.** End-points are $P(3, 4, 3)$, $Q(1, 1, -3)$; length is $|PQ| = 7$;
equations are: $\dfrac{x-1}{2} = \dfrac{y-1}{3} = \dfrac{z+3}{6}$. **64.** (i) Point $(1, 1, -1)$, (ii) $\varnothing$.
65. Vertices $(0, 0, 0)$, $(1, 0, 0)$, $(\frac{1}{2}, \frac{1}{2}, 0)$, $(\frac{1}{2}, \frac{1}{2}, \frac{1}{2})$.
66. $x^2+y^2+(2-y)^2 = 6$, i.e. $x^2+2y^2-4y-2 = 0$.
67. (i) $r = 1$, (ii) $r = 1/\sin\theta = \operatorname{cosec}\theta$, $0 < \theta < \pi$, (iii) $\{r = 0\}\cup\{\theta = \frac{1}{4}\pi\}\cup\{\theta = \frac{3}{4}\pi\}$ gives the right-circular cone, (iv) plane is the y-axis together with the points given by $\tan\phi = 1$, i.e. $\phi = \frac{1}{4}\pi$ or $\frac{5}{4}\pi$, (v) $r = 1/\cos\theta = \sec\theta$, $0 \leqslant \theta < \frac{1}{2}\pi$ $\big(\theta = 0$ giving the point (0, 0, 1)$\big)$.
69. $x = \frac{2}{3}$, $a = \frac{1}{3}$, $b = -\frac{2}{3}$, $c = -\frac{2}{3}$.
70. $x = \frac{1}{3}(2\xi+2\eta+\zeta)$, $y = \frac{1}{3}(2\xi-\eta-2\zeta)$, $z = \frac{1}{3}(-\xi+2\eta-2\zeta)$; $\xi^2+\eta^2-\zeta^2 = 1$, a hyperboloid of one sheet (of revolution about the ζ-axis).

Index

Index

addition of vectors, 52
additive property of orthogonal projection, 69, 70
angle between directions, 67
angle between two planes, 77
asymptotes of a hyperbola, 36, 37
axes, 4, 5, 45, 48

basis of vectors, 65
branches of a hyperbola, 35

canonical equation of an ellipse, 30, 31
———a hyperbola, 35
———a parabola, 27
centre of an ellipse, 30
——a hyperbola, 35
centroid of a tetrahedron, 87
———triangle, 7, 48, 63
change of coordinates, 19
circle centre $C(a, b)$, radius r, 11
closed half-planes, 18
common perpendicular of two lines, 80
component form of scalar product, 67, 68
———scalar triple product, 73
———vector product, 72
components of a vector, 56, 65
cone, 85, 86
conjugate axis of a hyperbola, 35
conjugate hyperbola, 35
coordinate brick, 46
coordinate planes, 46, 48
coordinate systems, 4, 5, 45, 81
coordinate unit vectors $\boldsymbol{i}, \boldsymbol{j}, \boldsymbol{k}$, 56
coordinates in a plane, 5
coordinates in 3-dimensional space, 45
coordinates on a line, 4
coplanar lines, 79
coplanar vectors, 62, 63
cylinders, 49, 85
—elliptic, hyperbolic, parabolic, 85
cylindrical polar coordinates, 81

definition of a conic, 26
dilatation, 24
directed line, 3
direction angles, 58
direction cosines and numbers, 58, 59, 60
directrix of a conic, 26
distance formula, 6, 46, 47
distributive property of scalar product, 68
———vector product, 72

eccentricity of a conic, 26
ellipse, 26, 29
ellipsoid, 83
elliptic paraboloid, 84
equality of vectors, 52
equation of a locus, 10
equations in symmetric form for a line 61
equations of lines, 12, 60, 61, 62
euclidean plane, 3
EUCLID's parallel postulate, 9
exterior of a circle, 11
———sphere, 49

fixed point of a transformation, 22
focal distance property of the ellipse, 31, 32
—————hyperbola, 36
focus of a conic, 26
fundamental properties of an ellipse, 29
———a hyperbola, 34

generators of a cylinder, 49
geometrical representation of vectors, 52
geometrical transformations, 21
gradient of a straight line, 7, 8

half-planes, 16, 17
homogeneous linear equations, 22
hyperbola, 26, 34
hyperbolic paraboloid, 85
hyperboloid of one sheet, 84
hyperboloid of 2 sheets, 84

interior of a circle, 11
———sphere, 49
intersection of line and plane, 78, 79
isometry, 24

latus rectum of an ellipse, 30
———a hyperbola, 35
———a parabola, 27
length of a vector, 51
line of intersection of two planes, 77, 78
line-segment, 3, 51
linear dependence and independence, 65
linear equation, 12, 75
linear programming, 16, 18
locus, 10, 48

magnitude of a vector, 51
major axis of an ellipse, 30
measure of a line-segment, 3
midpoint, 7, 58
minor axis of an ellipse, 30
multiplication of a vector by a scalar, 54

non-coplanar vectors, 62, 64, 65
non-homogeneous linear equations, 22
non-zero vector, 51
normal vector, 74

oblique axes, 5
octants, 46
open circular disc, 11
open half-planes, 18
origin, 4, 45
orthogonal matrix, 24
orthogonal projection, 69
orthonormal set of vectors, 68, 92

pair of planes, 85
parabola, 26, 27
parabolic mirror property, 29
parameter, 61
parametric equations for the ellipse $x^2/a^2 + y^2/b^2 = 1$, 33
—————hyperbola $x^2/a^2 - y^2/b^2 = 1$, 38
—————hyperbola $xy = c^2$, 42
—————line, 61
—————parabola $y^2 = 4ax$, 28
perpendicular distance from a point to a line, 13
——plane, 75, 76
plane sections, 83
point circle, 11
point sphere, 49
polar coordinates, 20
polar equation of ellipse, 32, 33
position ratio, 6
position vector, 55
principal axes of an ellipsoid, 83
projection of a line on a plane, 78
properties of addition of vectors, 53
——scalar multiples of vectors, 55

quadrants, 5
quadric surfaces, 83

rectangular axes, 5
rectangular hyperbola, 37, 42
reflection in a line OL, 23
right-handed systems, 45, 70, 71
rotation about O through angle α, 23
rotation of axes, 20, 82, 83

saddle point, 85
scalar equation of a plane, 74, 75
scalar multiples of vectors, 54, 55
scalar product, 67, 68
scalar triple product, 71
second focus of an ellipse, 31
———a hyperbola, 35
section formulae, 6, 7, 47, 57
shortest distance between lines, 79, 80, 81
signed volume of parallelepiped, 71
skew lines, 80

sphere, 48, 49
spherical polar coordinates, 81, 82
subsets of the plane, 10
surfaces of revolution, 86
symmetry of an ellipse, 31
——a hyperbola, 35
——a parabola, 27

tangent function, 8
tangent of angle which *AC* makes with *AB*, 14, 15
three-dimensional geometry, 45
translation of axes, 19, 82
translation (transformation), 22
transverse axis of a hyperbola, 35
triangle inequality, 6, 54

unit vectors, 55

vector bases, 64, 65
vector equation for a line, 60, 61
————plane, 63
vector product, 70
vector triple product, 73
vectors, 51
vertex of a parabola, 27
vertices of an ellipse, 30
——a hyperbola, 35

zero vector, 51